Call Me Perfect

BY: Your Inner Self

Copyright © 2017 by Natalie Grigson

Blah
Blah

Natalie Grigson
604 West 12ᵗʰ St.

table of Contents

You	1
Once upon a time there was a girl named Margery	3
Margery Tomlinson	3
Middle School: WHAT IS HAPPENING!!	4
Thoughts of Pizza	10
A Plan	12
OMG, You Look Great!	16
PAUSE	19
Girl Talk	20
Guys and Girls	20
Plus, it's Not Good for You	21
And Now, Back to the Show	22
Models in Bikinis	23
So Far Away	24
Does this sound familiar?	27
Morning Meltdown	29
Are You Okay?	31
FINE.	36
Finding Stillness	37
Extracurriculars	40
It's Like Chess Club... But Not.	43
Onto the Guys	49
CBT	51
Homework	57
Brain Food	59
Meeting Number Two	60
Sharing is Caring. And Crying. Lots of Crying.	62
Spaghetti Squash and Sentence Stems	66
Oh Yeah, You're Funny	70
Love and Mashed Potatoes	72
Slumber Party	74
Triggering	77
Appreciation Yo	79

You Gotta Be Kidding Me   83
CUPCAKES!   89
Now It's Time to Cry-A Lot   91
Happy General Holiday Season!   92
And They All Lived Happily Ever After... For the Most Part   97
Extras, Whatnots, And General Whozits   103
Body Scanning Meditation   105
Body Gratitude Meditation   106
Self-Love Meditation   107
Don't Numb That Negativity Meditation   108
Negativity Scribble Pages   110
Journal Pages   113
Cognitive Behavioral Therapy   125
Containment Box   130
A Letter to Your Body   131
A Letter from Your Body   132
A Letter to Food   133
A Letter from Food   134
Mirror, Mirror Exercise   135
List of Body Gratitudes   136
Authentic Relating Games   138
Some Sentence Stems   142
Healthy Food Stuff For Real   144
Oh Yeah... That Awkward Page About Puberty...   151
Consent   153
Manly Men: So 10 Years Ago   154
Stuff Smart People Have Said   156

YOU

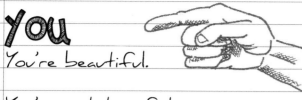

You're beautiful.

You're not too fat,

And you're not too skinny.

Your skin is just fine (yes, really.)

And even if sometimes you feel like you have to be perfect—you have to go on a diet, you have to be prettier, more handsome, stronger, less gangly, taller, have better ears—whatever—

YOU are already perfect, just as you are.

Now, I'm sure you've heard these things before—maybe from your parents or a teacher. And I'm sure you've heard the opposite before—that you're fat, ugly, unlovable, not good enough. Maybe you've heard it from kids at school, from the messages you get every day from television or magazines, or even from yourself when you look in the mirror.

I know that you've heard them before, because all this time, I've been here with you—your Inner Self—just listening.

Hello!

I'm Is. Some of you guys might have met me before when I introduced myself in a little book called *Just Call Me Is* (clever title, I know.) It was an introduction to mindfulness, which don't worry, I'll get into plenty here.

This time, though, I thought we'd take a different tack. Because as your Inner Self, I am also the Inner Self of oh, just like, everybody else in the world. See, we are all made up of the same stuff: energy. It's your soul, your consciousness, The Universe—whatever you want to call it, it's energy. It's me. It's you. It's that kid in your class that laughs really loud; it's the girl you think is so pretty that it hurts; it's everyone.

And as your Inner Self, I know that body image is on your mind A LOT. Just as much as it was on Margery's mind (who you'll meet in a minute.) Just as it's on the kid in your class's mind, and even on the mind of the prettiest girl in school.

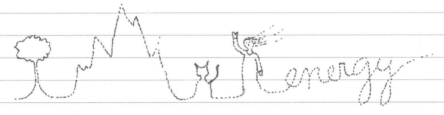

So, you and me—we're gonna have a talk about it. Don't worry, no one else needs to read this, or the notes that you make in the back of the book. And don't worry, I won't tell anyone that this is something you're struggling with.

But just know, you are NOT alone. More kids struggle with thoughts like "I am too fat" or "I'm not good looking enough" than anything else. Believe me, I know.

Especially kids like Margery.

And this is how her story goes.

Once upon a time there was a girl named Margery

Okay, okay. I won't bore you with the intro, because these "Once Upon a Times" tend to end with "Happily Ever Afters," and that, as we know, isn't always the case. Now, for those of you who read *Just Call Me Is*, the name Margery might sound a little familiar. As you'll remember, she was Tori's best friend in England, before Tori moved away.

And for those of you who *didn't* read *Just Call Me Is*, and have no idea what I'm talking about—don't sweat it. All you really need to know is that while I am your Inner Self, and Tori's Inner Self, I am also Margery's Inner Self. So while we followed Tori's story when she moved off to New York, there was still a story going on in England with Margery.

And so that is where we'll begin.

Margery Tomlinson

Margery Tomlinson grew up in a small town several hours outside of London. Her mom and dad split when she was just four-years-old, so like many kids Margery's age, she grew up mostly with her Mom. (Her dad had moved to Connecticut when she was just six.)

When we last saw Margery, she and her best friend, Tori were just entering fifth year—when suddenly, Tori moved away to New York City, because her dad had gotten a new job.

It was hard for Margery; harder than she let anyone

believe. Because, you see, Margery liked to play things cool; stay tough. She didn't like to ask for help. And she certainly didn't want anyone to see her cry. (Sound familiar?)

But cry she did, for several weeks after her best friend moved away. She spent much of her fifth-year, sitting by herself at lunch, eating cookies, reading at home, and hanging out with her Mom—whose main interests included pouring over fashion magazines, exercising constantly, and dating men half her age.

I'M CYNTHIA!

But we'll talk more about Cynthia later.

Our story truly begins several months after Tori left town: when Margery started secondary school. Or, as you in the U.S. might know it: Middle School.

Dun... Dun... Dun...

Just kidding. I'm sure you've heard the horror stories about Middle School (and you might even be in the middle of one yourself.) And yes, sometimes these years are rough—but not for everyone. Only for, you know, boys. And girls. And anyone in between. Okay, pretty much everyone.

There's just a lot is going on during these years. And Margery was about to find out about it firsthand.

Middle School: what is happening!!

The halls of Keating Secondary School were wide and lined with blue lockers, some open while their owners rifled through them, pell-mell, looking for books. Kids were everywhere—where there were maybe a hundred kids at her last school, there were at least six times as many here. They were calling back and forth to each other, running down the halls, giving each other high fives and hugs. It was like they all knew each other, and somehow Margery had missed the invite to the club.

On that first day of school, all the hundreds of students were crowded into the cafeteria to hear an announcement from the Headmaster, Mr. Pitts. Margery was sitting at a long wooden table with her other homeroom classmates— she only recognized four of them from the previous year.

"Hello, and welcome everyone to another great year at Keating Secondary School!"

Scattered applause. A few people were still talking.

"Now, as I'm sure you all know, every year at Keating is a chance to begin again. Whether you didn't do as well last year as you wanted to, or you did, or maybe you didn't make the friends, or go to the school dance with who you wanted to—"

At this, Mr. Pitts winked exaggeratedly and put his hands on his hips.

"I bet Mr. Pitts doesn't get to dance with anyone he wants to," someone whispered from just next to Margery. She turned her head—it was a boy with mousy brown hair, a long, narrow nose, and a football t-shirt on. "His stomach's sticking out so far, he probably can't even tie his shoes, let alone dance!" The boy and the one next to him,

Timothy Edwards, sniggered quietly.

Margery was saved having to respond when she realized that the mousy boy was only talking to the other boy. She turned around quickly, embarrassed somehow, and looked back up to the front where Mr. Pitts continued to talk.

But she wasn't paying attention anymore. She was looking at Mr. Pitts now, in a way she hadn't before.

Sure, he was a bit round around the middle—like she remembered her dad having been—and yeah, he had a chin more than most. But he seemed genuinely nice; like he really cared about the students and his school.

The boys continued to whisper rude things, occasionally bursting into quiet laughter, and finally, Margery turned in her seat and glared.

"What are you looking at, chubby?" Timothy Edwards snapped, smirking at her, braces shining.

And that was all it took.

Margery turned back in her seat toward the front, her eyes glazed over and her cheeks heating up. She was no longer hearing Mr. Pitts; she was hardly even aware when the bell rang for class. She forced herself not to cry.

Now hold up.

If you're thinking "That was rude! Why would someone say that to someone else?" I can tell you, because like I said, I'm everyone's Inner Self all at once. It's a big job, I tell you.

Now it's probably different for everyone, but in this case, Timothy Edwards was feeling really uncomfortable. He had just gotten his braces on and was feeling insecure. Plus, things at home were rocky. He was deeply unhappy, and for just a moment, he thought he could make himself feel a little better by making fun of Mr. Pitts. By making Margery feel bad.

Now as you may or may not know already, this thing that *thinks* it will feel better by making fun of others—that's not really you. We'll call it your Ego. It's the part of you that feels insecure, that worries, or even feels better than other people. It's the part of you that thinks about the past or frets about the future.

And it's the part of Margery that, as soon as Timothy called her chubby, thought—

Maybe I am.

Margery stayed late at school that first day for choir practice, and by the time she got home she was starving. Her mom was bustling around in the kitchen, a radio on the counter turned up loud, singing along to Madonna, and chopping up vegetables. Margery stood in the doorway for a minute and just watched her—shorter than most moms, but petite. She had strong arms and legs, a small waist, and her dark brown skin was smooth (not dotted with pimples, like Margery's was beginning to be.) When she saw Margery standing in the doorway, she shimmied her athletic body over to her, and grabbed her hands to dance.

"When all else fails and you long to be... Something better... uh, something, something. I know a place where you can get away... dance floor, and here's what it's for! Come on — Vogue. Let your body move to the music!

"Marge, you're not moving to the music!" her mom said, after Margery refused to play along. She stepped back and looked at her daughter.

"What's wrong? How did school go?"

And that's when Margery lost it. She had tried not to cry—she rarely even cried in front of her mother, because secretly, she thought her mom had enough to deal with being a single parent and all. But she couldn't keep the tears in any longer, and before she knew it, she was telling her mom all about what "that jerk" said at school.

(HER WORDS, NOT MINE.)

Now Cynthia wasn't always the most sensitive of people, let alone moms. As a kid, she grew grew up in a military home. She was always moving around. She barely saw her dad, Margery's grandad, and had been taught to have a "stiff upper lip" and "be tough." She was bullied as a kid for her dark skin and black, curly hair—different than most of the girls' in her school at the time—and she'd protected herself by closing herself off.

Usually, she encouraged Margery to do the same thing; even if she didn't mean to. What I mean is, just the way she acted changed the way Margery thought she should act.

You're a smart kid, and I'm sure you've seen this all the time. Other kids taking on their parents' religious beliefs, their political thoughts, even how they think they should eat or exercise or feel about their bodies. So Margery tried to stay tough, like her mom.

But this time, Cynthia rushed forward and scooped Margery into a hug, so tight, it felt like she'd never let go. Margery needed it so badly, and she didn't even know it. She cried and cried into her mom's shoulder, making a big wet mark on her sleeve. She cried for the day at school. She cried for her best friend moving away. She cried for things she didn't even know she felt, like her dad leaving; like her mom's pain. When she had no more tears to cry, she sat down at the dinner table heavily, dropping her backpack on the floor.

"I know what it's like to be bullied," her mom told her as she put their dinner plates on the table. Her mom had a big bowl filled with spinach, broccoli florets, tomatoes, and what looked to Margery like dried pond scum.

(It was seaweed.)

At twelve-years-old, of course, Margery preferred spaghetti and garlic bread to what she called "tortoise salads," and dug in hungrily (crying is hard work!), twirling the noodles around her fork. As her mom told her about her own childhood—moving from place to place; always the new girl; always different for the color of her skin—a strange feeling came over Margery. Something wasn't quite right, and she knew it didn't have anything to do with her mother's story.

By the time she had finished her small cup of vanilla ice cream for dessert, she realized what it was. It was a simple, yet destructive little thought—

I shouldn't have eaten that.

thoughts of Pizza

School had been in session for about two weeks. It had been two weeks of homework, two weeks of meeting new classmates from the other primary schools, and two weeks of actually feeling a little bit better for Margery. After that first day, she avoided Timothy and Connor (the mousy boy) like gum on the sidewalk, and even felt a little bit more confident. She'd met a girl named Emma in Choir. She was a waif of a girl— thin with blonde, wispy hair and watery blue eyes. She looked like she could just blow away or dissolve into the air, Margery thought.

But she liked spending time with Emma... even if it did make her feel, well, a bit bigger. Emma was goofy and weird; she didn't apologize for who she was, and she encouraged Margery to be herself—to speak up in classes, to tell jokes. And to her own surprise, it turned out Margery was pretty funny.

One day during the third week of school, Margery and Emma were bringing their trays from the lunch line back to a table. They'd taken to sitting with a group of other Choir kids—boys and girls from their year and a couple of years older as well. Unfortunately for Margery, Mouse Boy Connor was one of them.

"Hey Emma," Connor said almost as soon as they sat down. He didn't even look at Margery. "You know, I know someone who has a crush on you."

Emma just raised an eyebrow and picked up her piece of pizza. Before she took a bite, she used a spoon to slather the whole thing heartily with thick, creamy Ranch dressing.

Margery's stomach growled.

"Yeah, more like a few people who have a crush on you," Connor went on. "Wow—you eat like my brother! He has to eat like a whole ton, cuz he's on the football team," he said, watching as Emma pretty much inhaled her piece of pizza, then another. He looked over at Margery, noticing her for the first time, as though to say *Pretty impressive, right?*

She was just raising her pizza to her own mouth—a single slice covered in veggies, instead of ranch dressing—and he barked out a laugh.

"Oh, that's why. Maybe you should think about giving your pizza to Emma the Champion Eater over here; get yourself a salad instead."

And without waiting for a reply, Connor got up and walked back to the other end of the table. He sat down next to a tall, popular, boy with dark skin and black hair that Margery recognized as Vince Crowley, and the two started whispering and laughing, occasionally looking her way.

Margery dropped her gaze and put down her pizza.

"Oh, come on, Margery," Emma said, looking across at her and the at the guys. "You can't let that [CENSORED*] get to you. He's just jealous that you're the funniest person in our class and he's not."

*What? I can totally do that.

When Margery still refused to finish her lunch, Emma resignedly ate it for her, lest it be thrown away.

"You can't throw out good pizza," she said, stuffing her face.

Margery watched Emma chomp down on the last bite of pizza; ranch dressing smeared all over her face. She looked like a toddler. Still, Margery wished she could eat like that and be so skinny (maybe minus the mess). But she was naturally thicker than Emma. She had a waist, she had a tummy, and by God, she had a butt! She wasn't unhealthy, but she wasn't a string bean or a runway model either.

She was perfect.

But, as you probably guessed (and can relate), she didn't see it that way. Not at all.

a Plan

Over the next few days, Margery's Ego went into overdrive. It was feeling pretty bruised and banged up from what Connor said, and so naturally, it made Margery feel this way, too.

She was overwhelmed with thoughts.

I'm too fat.

I'm ugly.

No one likes me.

I'm alone.

And on and on her thoughts went. Until the end of the week, when something changed.

_____

For the first time since Tori had moved away, Margery was going to have a sleepover. Without the pressure of the other kids at school around, Margery was feeling a little bit better and by the time the Emma actually got to her house Friday night, she was so excited, she wasn't even thinking about what Connor had said to her.

Her mom had pulled out all the stops for the slumber party, just excited that Margery had found a new, good friend—who, in Margery's mom's words was "just so pretty!"

Their usually pristine living room looked like a nest for teenage girls. There was a stack of movies next to the big T.V. on the far wall; strewn across the coffee table were boxes of pizza, carrots and dip, chips and salsa. The big blue and white striped couch was piled with pillows and blankets. Her mom had even cancelled her date with Rafael in order to be home with Margery and Emma.

Things were looking up. And as the girls went to Margery's room and talked about school and friends (Emma had also recently lost a best friend, Jake, who still went to their school, but was suddenly too cool), and then even when they trouped into the living room to watch a movie, things were just getting better. If it wasn't for what happened over dinner, it might just have gone off without a hitch.

"Wow!" Margery's mom, Cynthia, exclaimed, looking across the living room coffee table. Margery, her mom, and Emma were all sitting on the floor around the wooden table, the box of pizza open in the middle. Margery and Emma were on their second slices (and going on thirds, it looked like, for Emma), while Cynthia was busying herself with a salad and slice of pink salmon. "Emma, you must have a metabolism like a humming bird. Do you work out?"

Margery rolled her eyes. Working out was one of those things, like juice cleanses and high heeled boots, that her mom could just go on and on about.

Emma just shrugged though, and through a full mouth said, "I don't know. I guess I play around outside a lot, but..."

"You're just so thin! I wish I could eat like that and stay so thin. Don't get me wrong, I love to hit the gym, but sometimes I just really miss eating pizza. Of course, I still want to lose five pounds, so pizza is out of the question for me," her mom laughed, then looked sadly down at her salmon. In that moment, Margery wanted to pluck it from her plate and throw it out the window. "Oh well—there's nothing that tastes so good as being skinny looks, right?"

- 14 -

Emma looked at her, completely baffled, and then grabbed another slice of pizza.

Margery, on the other hand, put down her nearly finished slice and wiped her greasy fingers on a paper napkin.

"I think I'm going to grab some carrots," she said, casually. She got up and left the room, heading toward the kitchen, totally missing her mom's confused, if not pleasantly surprised, look, and Emma's look of sadness.

To be clear, Margery's mom, Cynthia, had never actually suggested that Margery should lose weight. She'd never said anything about her daughter's metabolism being too slow, or her daughter needing to lose five pounds. In fact, she'd always allowed Margery to eat mostly what she liked (even if she, herself, was eating salads almost all the time.) But the things she *didn't* say about Margery—you're healthy, you're smart, you're funny, you've got so much going on for you!—well, they spoke just as loudly.

And even if she didn't say things like "Margery, you need to lose weight," being around her mom's constant dieting, and seeing the way Cynthia looked at herself in the long, ornately carved mirror in the hall—pinching the tiny bit of fat on her stomach and frowning—it sent the message loud and clear:

Margery was fat. And that wasn't okay.

So, Margery made a plan. That very night, she decided that she was done eating foods for pleasure. She loved the occasional pizza or cookie (who doesn't?), but to her, these foods were now off limits. Until she went to school and people looked at her the way they looked at Emma;

until her mom remarked about how thin she was, she was eating tortoise salads, too.

Now, I don't think I need to tell you how ridiculous this plan was. You know already that different people have different body types. Some people, like Emma, are naturally stick thin. Maybe they will be forever; but probably when they hit the big P word, their bodies will change. (You know the one: Puberty. Don't worry—we'll get to that later.)

Some people, like Margery, are curvier. Some people spend their whole lives swinging back and forth on diets, like Cynthia, and really have no idea what their natural weight is like.

But Margery didn't know how exhausting her new Plan would be. And she certainly didn't know how harmful it would become.

OMG, You Look Great!

Margery had been in school for almost two months, and had been on her Plan for about four weeks. She'd started out by grabbing one of her mom's diet books the day after her slumber party, while her mom was at her double Pilates class.

That afternoon she poured over it for hours while outside it rained and rained. She made notes, created a meal plan, and even wrote down what times she would eat throughout the day. She wrote down a total amount of fat per day, and the total number of calories.

Margery's Ego was as happy as a dog playing fetch, because all the sudden, it had a job. It was thinking, "Oh good! If I just follow this plan, I will be skinny, and everyone will like me, and I'll be happy forever! Horray! Unicorns and rainbows!"

Of course, I was just sitting back and watching the whole thing; quietly waiting for her to slow down enough to notice me.

But she didn't. Margery was too busy paying attention to her Ego, thinking that dieting would give her what she truly wanted. Well, we all know how that goes.

_____

"Oh Em Gee," a pale and freckled girl with bushy red hair half-shouted. She was marching directly up to Margery's seat in the cafeteria. Both of her hands were on her hips and her lips were parted in a comical "O." She tried to place her—Ali? Abby? Girl who always skips gym class?—but before she could so much a remember her name, the girl had descended upon her like a gangly bird of prey.

"You look so great! I've been out of school for, like, two weeks—my parents took us to Elba Island on holiday—and now I see you, and my gosh! I just can't believe it! You're not fat anymore!"

She smiled hugely, showing a row of pearly white teeth, probably thinking she'd paid Margery a big complement.

Margery just stared.

"Keep this up and by Christmastime, you'll be skinny!"

And with that, the girl turned and walked away toward the lunch line, her red hair bouncing in time with her steps. Just then, Emma walked over, and set her tray down. It was laden with lasagna, spinach salad, and a sliced apple.

"What was Abby Chalmers doing over here?" she asked, already picking up a forkful of cheesy lasagna. She stared after Abby (Abby!) as she walked away. "That girl isn't very nice."

Margery glanced over to where Abby was currently shouting at a short blonde boy in the lunch line, then at Emma who was scooping lasagna into her mouth unashamedly. Her stomach growled.

"I don't know. I mean, she said she thinks I look great," Margery mumbled. She looked down at her journal and made some notes.

Emma was staring across the table, watching what Margery was writing. She put her fork down and sighed.

"Margery, are you okay? It seems like you're putting in a whole lot of work into this diet thing, and it doesn't seem like you're even feeling very good..."

"That's not true! I feel great, better than ever!" Margery said quickly, as she snapped her notebook shut. The truth was, Margery did not feel great, better than ever. She felt terrible.

She was constantly hungry—her mouth watered when she even thought about food. Her grades had started to gradually get worse, because she couldn't think. Her brain was constantly foggy. She hadn't been speaking up in class as much. It was like she was disappearing altogether.

But she still had work to do. She wanted to lose just five more pounds. Just five more pounds and she'd be happy.

Pause

Dear Reader,

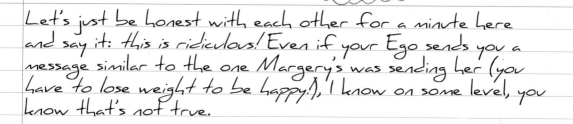

Uh. I don't think that's how it works.

Let's just be honest with each other for a minute here and say it: *this is ridiculous!* Even if your Ego sends you a message similar to the one Margery's was sending her (you have to lose weight to be happy!), I know on some level, you know that's not true.

And on that same level, you *know* that dieting like this is unhealthy. It's called "crash dieting" for a reason. You cut out all sorts of food groups, and for a while you might lose a little weight. Woo hoo! How fun!

BUT, you're also losing important brain function. Your body needs a healthy balance of all the food groups, including healthy fats. You need a certain amount of calories per day, just in order to keep your body working, your heart beating, and your lungs breathing. In other words, it takes food just to keep you alive!

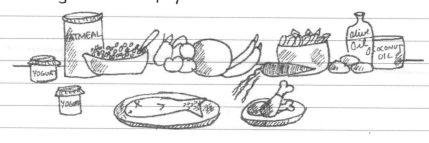

Plus, your body needs to have a certain amount of fat in order to simply function! Girls: this part's for you. Guys reading, you can follow along to learn some fun facts! But if girl stuff freaks you out, feel free to skip this part.

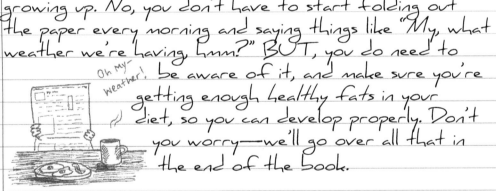

girl talk

Alright ladies: let's talk puberty. I know, I just went there. It got weird. But this is important. Your bodies need to have a certain amount of body fat (it is HEALTHY, I repeat HEALTHY) in order to have periods. That's why a lot of girls, anywhere from ages 8-15, start to get bigger lips, and thighs, and waists, and butts, and stomachs, and boobs. You know, all that fun stuff.

It can be totally confusing, but it just means you're growing up. No, you don't have to start folding out the paper every morning and saying things like "My, what weather we're having, hmm?" BUT, you do need to be aware of it, and make sure you're getting enough healthy fats in your diet, so you can develop properly. Don't you worry—we'll go over all that in the end of the book.

Oh My- Weather!

guys and girls

Okay, guys, you back with me? Girls? This part's for everyone—and yes, it's still about puberty so, yes, it's going to be a little awkward for a minute. (Puberty is awkward.)

It's important to know that everyone goes through puberty at totally different times. Some guys will grow about two feet in a year, while their friends are still shorter than the girls. Some guys' voices will drop dramatically and sound like Darth Vader's. Some won't. Everyone goes through it, but at different times.

Whether you're a guy or girl, though, puberty comes whenever it is ready to come for you. And when it does— it's going to do some crazy stuff to your body. More muscle, more fat, more pimples (for sure), hair... you know all about that. (And if you don't, we'll talk more in the back of the book). The important thing is: It's natural. Your body is supposed to change. So dieting to keep your ten-year-old body ain't gonna work.

Plus, it's Not good for you

Not only will this sort of dieting make you feel bad, but it doesn't work. Yep. Dieting in the way that Margery was going about it, might make you lose weight for a little while, but it doesn't and cannot last. The weight will come back (and maybe more), plus, it's really unhealthy for your health to swing back and forth all the time with weight.

So if a doctor has told you that you need to lose weight for health reasons, it's better to just develop healthy eating habits that you can keep around for the rest of your life. And no, this will never look like starving yourself. And yes, you can most certainly still eat the foods you enjoy— including the occasional cookie. In fact, I'll even include a whole list of healthy foods that are good for your body and development in the back of the book. But I repeat: dieting won't help.

But you're smart. I bet you knew that already.

and now, back to the Show

Margery continued down what was clearly becoming a pretty unhealthy spiral. She did exactly what she said she'd do in her journal and she felt miserable. Her hair was getting stringy and dry, her skin was cracked, her face was breaking out worse than ever, and she couldn't concentrate to save her life. After another month, she did lose those five pounds, and she still felt miserable.

So, of course, she thought she had to keep going. Lose more weight.

Every day after getting home from school, she felt exhausted. Starving. She couldn't think. She would curl up in the living room, barely making a dent in the big, cushy striped sofa. She'd wrap up in a blanket and watch T.V. and read her mom's Cosmos and Marie Claires, too exhausted to concentrate on her homework.

She'd stare longingly at the women gracing the magazines' pages. They were all so thin. Their legs looked about as long as Margery was tall. Their hair, as they strutted down runways, or even stood in photos on the beach in bikinis, seemed to wave out behind them like the wind was blowing it wildly. They looked so happy. So beautiful.

But to tell you the truth—it was all a lie.

Models in bikinis

I know what you're thinking—it is not a lie that these women are beautiful! How could they not be happy?

Here's the deal: the women that you see in magazines, online, on television, or in movies; these women who look so beautiful and thin and happy! Well, they might be happy, and they might not be happy. But it doesn't have anything to do with what they look like.

I know you've heard it before, but happiness comes from the inside. It might be cheesy, but it's true.

Take miss Bethany, for example, the woman Margery just happened to be looking at in the latest edition of Cosmo Magazine.

The day of this photo shoot—it was an advertisement for bathing suits, shot on the beach—she was told over and over how great she looked. Stunning! And so thin! The director of the shoot told her, the makeup team told her. But it barely sunk in, because Bethany was staring at herself in the mirror, just at the little layer of fat still left on her stomach. She hated it. She hated herself.

And so she didn't eat all day.

While the "beautiful" pictures were being taken, she stood knee-deep in the freezing cold water, waves lapping up against her and getting sand in places sand really shouldn't be. She was shivering, hungry, and light-headed, all the while thinking that if she only didn't have that little layer of fat on her stomach, she'd be happy. She wasn't, but she smiled for the camera anyway.

By the time the photo was printed and in Margery's hands, Bethany's appearance had undergone a complete transformation. Her skin was much tanner and smoother; the few bumps on her face had been fixed; her eyes were no longer brown, but a brilliant blue/green like the ocean behind her; and the little layer of fat on her stomach had been removed, as well as about two inches from her thighs and hips.

ORIGINAL PHOTO   WHAT YOU SEE

The picture had been totally Photoshopped, you see.

So what Margery stared at that day, so longingly, willing her body to be just like this one, was not real at all. And even if it was real, the model herself was insecure about her body*. Of course I only know this because (duh) I also happen to be Bethany's Inner Self.

Unfortunately, Margery didn't know this.

So she kept on with her Plan.

*I'm not saying that all models are insecure about their bods. There are quite a few who are totally confident. BUT, let me tell you, it doesn't have to do with the way they look. It's how they feel—and that can only come from within.

So far away

The next day at school went by in a blur. Faces passing in the hallway, people talking, time in classes trickling by slowly and then speeding up in large jumps. Margery felt like she was starting to lose it. She simply couldn't focus.

But she couldn't seem to stop.

When she got home after school, there was a frozen lasagna thawing on the counter and a note:

I'm working late tonight. Left you your favorite—see you when I get home!
  -Mum

EAT ME!
DO IT!
DO IT!

Margery stared at the lasagna. Layers of ricotta cheese, tomato sauce, chicken, spinach, mushrooms, garlic, and oregano, all neatly between perfectly puffed strips of thick pasta. She was beyond hungry—her stomach ached. Yet, she couldn't bring herself to eat it. Rather than let her mom know she was

Noooooo

starving herself, though, she took the lasagna out of the freezer and threw it in the dumpster outside. She vaguely wondered how long she could keep this up as she walked back into the house. She was dizzy.

"It's okay, I'll just have some carrots." She grabbed some carrots and hummus. All the while, her stomach felt like it was tying itself in knots—she was so hungry. I mean, I don't even eat, but I can tell you, I wanted her to eat a sandwich or something!

But, of course, Margery wasn't listening to me. She was so far away from me, stuck in this disordered eating and thinking, she might as well have been on the moon.

The next morning, Margery's mom came into the kitchen

NOT A BALANCED BREAKFAST

where Margery was pouring herself a glass of grapefruit juice for breakfast. She'd just finished her homework and it was still sitting out on the table.

Margery's mom, as usual, was bustling around the kitchen, hurried to make the long commute to the hospital (their town was so small, the nearest hospital was in the next city over.) However, when she saw Margery—seemingly for the first time in months—she stopped.

"Hey Margey." She didn't seem to know what to say. "Do you want some breakfast? I was just going to grab a protein bar on the way out the door, but I can whip something up really quick." She crossed the room and opened the pantry. "Maybe some oatmeal?"

Margery felt annoyed and touched at the same time. The idea of her mom "whipping something up" before going to work was so novel, she couldn't dare refuse. It was a simple but thoughtful offer. But the idea of eating oatmeal (at which her brain screamed: oatmeal! OMG, how many calories will that be? I bet there's brown sugar and butter in it, too!) terrified her.

See, until this very morning, Margery had mostly managed to avoid mealtimes with her mom—Cynthia was almost always either at work or out doing something else. And at first, Margery's mom had commented on just how good—how fit!—how slim!—she was looking. But something in the way her mom was looking at her now, told her she was worried.

So once again, her Ego took the reins:

Fine! She's just jealous because I'm getting so skinny, she thought. She can worry all she wants, but she always said Emma was pretty. I'm just getting to be as thin as her.

But instead her mouth, and her stomach, said: "Yeah, okay."

Cynthia heated up some oats in a pan and added the signature dollop of butter and two spoonfuls of brown sugar, while quickly calling in to the E.R. to let them know she'd be a little late. (She was an office assistant, not a doctor, so relax.)

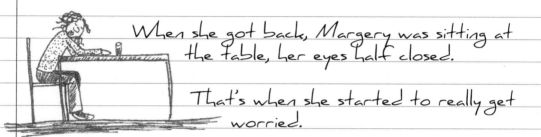

When she got back, Margery was sitting at the table, her eyes half closed.

That's when she started to really get worried.

She stood staring at her, her baby girl, wondering when she'd gotten so skinny; so unhealthy-looking. She remembered how she'd encouraged her at first, complementing her on losing some of that "baby fat" and even took her shopping to celebrate. She'd gone on a frenzy at the grocery store—buying up slim fast bars, lettuce, cucumbers, and all sorts of "tortoise" food, excited that Margery was losing weight. Or on a deeper level, perhaps she was just excited to share a similar hobby, for once, with her daughter: body obsession.

But now, as she looked at Margery, she wondered if she hadn't pushed her too hard.

does this sound familiar?

Because if it does, you're not alone. A lot of the reason kids like you struggle with body image is because your parents are where you learn everything first. I mean, they're your number one role models (whether you like it or not). So if you have a mom or dad or aunt or uncle or maybe you're being raised by wolves—whoever! If your parent figure is constantly on a diet, or worried about his or her weight, you might just pick that up from them.

Like Margery.

And plus, if your parent gets super excited about you losing weight, or tries to encourage you to lose weight, you might want to talk to them. Tell them I sent ya. In fact, just show them this:

Dear Parent,

First of all, congratulations. You have turned out an AMAZING kid. This kid is smart, funny, creative, imaginative, and absolutely beautiful. Well done.

Now, if you bought this book for your kiddo, or are aware that he or she's reading it, you probably know why. Maybe he or she is a little overweight. A little underweight. Likely, he or she is struggling in some way with appearance.

And who can blame them? It is EVERYWHERE these days. It's in the media, on social media, pressure from other kids at school, and—

Of course, at home.

Now I'm not trying to get on your back, parent. I mean, as I'm your kid's Inner Self, I'm also yours, and you and me, we're tight. But I do want to make you aware that what YOU do from here on matters far more than anything I could say. Your kids are going to watch your actions first (even if they don't admit it).

So if you're not happy with your body, chances are your kids are going to pick this up.

I'm not suggesting that you can magically just change your own body image issues overnight, but I am suggesting that you can work on it. And you can at least refrain from talking about dieting, weight loss, or appearance, whether it's yours, your child's, or someone else's. Because that stuff is hurting your kid.

And if you find yourself saying things like "Wow, you're beautiful!" or "You look so _____!" (fit, thin, lean, skinny, pretty, handsome, chubby, overweight, stocky, fat...), please try something that doesn't focus on what your child looks like. "You're so strong!" "You're so creative, I love the art that you make!" "You are such a talented storyteller!" "You seem so healthy!"

The point is, steer clear from talking appearance—especially with your kiddo who might be struggling with this. Focus on what an awesome little specimen they are. Focus on health. On happiness. But hey—we'll talk more at the end of the book. There will be a few exercises for parents and kids to do together.

And don't worry—you're rockin' this.

Morning Meltdown

After breakfast that morning, Margery's mom drove her to school (usually Margery walked). She kept glancing sideways at her, as though worried she'd just disappear.

Margery, meanwhile, couldn't stop thinking about the buttery, sweet, oatmeal she'd just eaten. Or rather, her Ego couldn't stop thinking about it.

I CAN'T BELIEVE YOU ATE THAT!

YOU'RE STUPID!

ALL THAT HARD WORK FOR NOTHING

YOU'RE A FAILURE!

YOU ARE SO FAT!

Sound familiar?

Of course it does. Many people who are struggling with body image have these sorts of thoughts all the live long day. It's SO EXHAUSTING. When you're thinking these things, I'm still there, watching all the while, quietly saying "Hey, wait! I'm here! You don't have to hurt yourself with these mean thoughts!"

And sometimes—sometimes!—you guys hear me. Maybe you sit down and meditate. Maybe you draw, or write in a journal, or sit in nature, climb a tree, or somehow just stop thinking long enough to feel my presence.

Unfortunately, this wasn't that kind of moment for Margery.

That morning after her mom dropped her off at school, she did something she'd never done before. She hurriedly waved goodbye over her shoulder, and rushed straight into the front doors, as her mom worriedly watched her spindly little legs. Just as her mom pulled away and was thinking she'd come home early that day to talk with her, Margery was bursting into a stall in the girl's bathroom, where she made herself throw up.

She spent the rest of first period in the bathroom crying. What had she done?

are you okay?

By the time Margery walked into her second period class, (Geography taught by Ms. Steppin), the students were already handing in their homework. Margery sat down, the little mascara she wore to school was stained down her cheeks like black rivers. Her eyes were puffy and red. She just looked down at the table top.

"Margery—is there a reason you're so,"

Ms. Steppin stopped talking, her lilting Welsh accent grounding to a halt. She was looking at Margery for the first time. Margery felt her eyes, as well as the eyes of (what she imagined) everyone else in the entire room—the entire school! The world! boring into her head. (Though, of course, the only person who was paying her any attention was Ms. Steppin.)

"Well, that's okay, dear. You can hand in the assignment at the end of class, so we can go ahead and get started with the lesson. Yes, yes, now where did I put my book..."

Ms. Steppin doddled off to the front of the room, looking here and there and occasionally muttering to herself. Margery was grateful for the distraction—everyone was paying attention to the teacher now, some whispering and giggling, some just staring agog, because simply put, Ms. Steppin was just so weird. As Margery wiped her cheeks with the back of her sleeves, she watched her curiously, like you might an odd bird.

She had long, long, wavy red hair that she usually wore behind her head with some sort of impractical tool—a pencil, a clothespin, once, a screwdriver. She had pale skin, freckles dotting her nose, and the greenest eyes Margery had ever

- 31 -

seen. And as Margery looked at her, she noticed her body—not skinny. But curved. Pear shaped. She realized then that Ms. Steppin was, in fact, quite beautiful. And she looked nothing like the women in her magazines.

"Ah ha! Here it is!" Ms. Steppin announced loudly to the class, holding up, not a book, but a sandwich. "I have been looking for this since yesterday. Now—" she tossed the sandwich out the open classroom window. "Let's talk about Romania."

Now if you're wondering why I don't take you through the lesson here and explain all the fun facts about Romania, it's not because I wasn't there or not listening. I'm always around. But the thing is, Margery was pretty checked out. Ever since she'd made herself throw up that oatmeal, her head felt like it was filled with thick fog and might just float away. She felt weird. She was totally out of it.

"Margery," Ms. Steppin said. Margery looked around, surprised to find the rest of the seats in class were empty. She must have dozed off. There was, however, a dark-skinned boy with a round inquisitive face hanging around sort of awkwardly at the doorway. He seemed to be busying himself looking at the doorframe.

"Did you do the homework?"

Margery shook her head. She'd forgotten.

"Okay. That's okay. I wanted to talk to you about something. Can you stay for a bit? I can write you a note for—"

"Health Class with Coach Michaels."

"Ah, right. Health class," Ms. Steppin said. Margery thought she caught her role her green, cat-like eyes a bit at this.

(She totally did.)

"Right. So Margery, I've noticed something changing about you."

Margery got excited. She knew where this was going—Yes! She's about to tell me how skinny I've gotten and how great I look! She's probably a talent agent on the side and wants me to model! Or to take up ballet, or dancing, or—

"I'm starting to get worried about your health."

Well that wasn't what she was expecting. She stared at her teacher.

"I don't want to make any assumptions, because as far as I know, you could be really sick with mono or something like that and have gotten so thin as a side effect. In which case, I'd like to talk to your mother.

"However, if you haven't been suffering with an illness, I wanted to let you know that if you're not eating enough, well... I've been there before myself, and I know how hard it can be. I wouldn't bring it up at all, but I've noticed your grades are slipping—not just in my class. Oh yes, I've talked to a few of your other teachers. And you're just looking so...

Thin! Beautiful! Skinny! Margery still hoped.

"So sick. I wanted to let you know that I can help you. That it doesn't have to be this way. In fact, there is a group meeting twice a week after school with several other students, myself, the counselor, Jordan who's waiting in the doorway... Jordan what are you doing?"

Margery's head was spinning. Her eyes went out of focus. She felt like she was in a full-on panic. Her thoughts were racing out of control, getting more and more defensive. She was vaguely aware that the boy, Jordan she thought, was still standing in the doorway, half glancing in the room nervously, half pretending to be looking at his watch. Ms. Steppin was still talking. Somewhere there was a clock ticking...

"No. No thank you. Like you said, I've just been sick. Mono. So, that's why I haven't been doing as well in school, and that's why I've lost a little weight. But really, I'm fine."

And with that, Margery got up, grabbed her backpack, and left the room, nearly bowling the boy in the doorway over as she huffed by.

———

As she walked down the hallway, kids laughing and rushing between classes swarming around her, her thoughts swarmed as chaotically in her head; a tornado of fear and denial.

She's just jealous of how skinny I've gotten, because she's so fat.

She just wants to be young and pretty again. She's totally not pretty. Why did I ever think so?"

And on and on her thoughts went. She was so in her head, she didn't even realize someone was calling her name.

"Margery!" She knew it was Emma before she saw her. A second later, Emma had stopped her roughly with her arm and spun her around. One look at Margery's face—splotchy and shining with anger—and Emma stopped smiling.

Before she knew it, Margery was telling Emma all about how unfair it was. How Ms. Steppin had totally just attacked her out of nowhere, suggesting that she was too skinny. When really, she was just totally jealous. And ugly, too.

Emma watched her friend, frowning. She didn't want to say anything, because she already saw how upset Margery was. But there was a little voice in her head, a very quiet feeling of what was right in this situation, that urged her to encourage her friend to get help. (You guessed it, it was ME!)

"I don't want to make things worse or anything, but... well, it seems to me like Ms. Steppin has a point. You just don't look healthy anymore."

Margery couldn't believe it. Her thoughts screamed at her friend—how dare she take Ms. Steppin's side! Maybe

Emma was jealous Margery was finally getting attention too!

But behind it all, she could hear my same little voice; that quiet calm saying "You know, she's right."

fine.

Just for the record, Margery was FINE. She kept telling anyone who asked—"Hey, how are you?" "You doing okay?" "Is anything wrong?"—she was FINE. Until she was so fed up with being asked, she said FINE, and simply decided to skip the rest of the day at school.

She'd never skipped a day in her life, so walking away from campus at around 1:30, the whole world felt foreign. She was seeing the town in a different light, literally. There were different people milling about on the little street next to her school, dotted with a café, a bakery, a small market, and a post office. People in slacks. People taking a break from work. A few older teenagers hanging around outside the café, eating lunch together and talking animatedly.

Her stomach growled as she neared them. She was so hungry she was ready to tear that bacon, lettuce, and tomato on rye right out of the blonde guy's hands. She must have stopped and started, because for a moment, the group paused and looked over at her, questioningly. Embarrassed, she kept on walking.

It was a small town, and a small street—on this side there were just a few businesses. Each had a sort of antiquey look—carved wooden door frames and details, richly painted faces and window frames. Normally she loved looking at these little dollhouse-like buildings. This day, however, she hardly knew they were there.

By the time she reached the end of the road, her head was foggy and she could think of nothing but food. She needed to eat; she knew it. And just as she was turning down Harrison Street toward her house, that's when it happened.

Her right foot was in front of her, stepping up onto the curb, and all the sudden, it was as though she was swimming deep under water. She couldn't tell up from down, her vision went black around the edges, and her head felt like it had simply floated away from her body, like a balloon.

Her last thought was to try to put her hands out in front of her to brace her fall, but the ground was coming up to meet her faster, her hands couldn't get there quick enough, and then—all was blackness.

finding Stillness

"...wasn't even supposed to be at home today, but I had been feeling a cold coming on..."

"...severely low EKG levels..."

"We'll have to keep her here overnight, at least, to monitor her... Her pulse is still weak, but the fluids seem to be helping..."

In and out, Margery drifted. She was dimly aware that she was in the hospital. There was no question—all around, she could hear little beeps from the monitors, people's voices coming in and out of the room. Occasionally, someone would move the IV in her arm around painfully, or squeeze her foot. Kiss her forehead.

And then she'd drift back...

To me.

It had been so long since Margery and I were really in touch—like, you know, hanging out on the reg—that it took something pretty drastic to get her thoughts to slow down enough for her to even notice me. Something like fainting.

And no, of course, I'm not advocating fainting to get in touch with me. I'm advocating meditation. Stillness. Writing in the journal pages in the back of this book. Drawing. Painting. Being in nature. But Margery had replaced the things that made her feel at peace with an addiction: namely, anorexia. And she'd forgotten all about her connection with that still space inside of her. With me.

And so it was that as she laid in that hospital bed, for the first time in months, she could feel a calm stillness inside her. Her thoughts were no longer racing; no longer telling her things like "You can't eat that!" "I can't believe you did eat that!" or "Look how pretty she is! If only I was that pretty, life would be easier..."

No. For the first time in months, her mind was quiet.

And from that quiet, still space, it was as though a voice spoke to her, though not with any words. It was more a feeling.

That feeling was: I need help. I surrender.

"Margery?"

It was her mom's voice, and Margery had a feeling she'd been saying it for a while. Her eyes fluttered open reluctantly, and there in front of her was her mom's face. Her dark brown eyes, mirrors of Margery's, were red and puffy; she'd clearly been crying.

"Oh, Margie! I'm so sorry! I feel like it's all my fault! I keep talking about how important it is to be thin, and I kept encouraging you to lose weight—but oh, Margie, it doesn't matter! None of that stuff matters, you know. As long as you're healthy and happy! I hate to say it, Marge, but I really think you might need help. I know you don't want to hear it, but really, I got a call from a teacher from your school this morning and I was going to talk to you about it after school, but then—"

"Mom. MOM!" Margery said, groggily. Her mom was crying again, hugging her daughter awkwardly, in a sort of choke hold. "I know. I need help."

At this, her mom sat up and wiped the tears away from her face. She looked a little confused at Margery's reaction, but then pulled herself together. "Oh, alright then. Well. How was the rest of your day?"

Margery smiled weakly, and half wished she was still asleep, but felt grateful for her mom's presence. She felt scared of what would come next—what would help look like? How much weight would she have to gain? Would people make fun of her? Maybe it was the almost hypnotic beeping of the machines, or maybe it was just having her mom there—actually there for her—but slowly, her worry started to drift away into peace. She listened, rather than talked, as her mom told her about a woman at work. Scared, but grateful, to still be there.

Extracurriculars

As it turned out, one of Margery's neighbors had been the one to find her completely unconscious on the ground down the street from her house. Niles Simmons must have called the house twenty times in the few days since Margery's hospital visit to check on her, each time telling Margery the story back to her, as if she didn't know.

"And I was just walking down the street with Princess Peony—she has a sensitive bladder, you know. Needs to go out at least every few hours, which makes it hard to have a long day at work without taking a lunch break, you see. But that day, I wasn't even at work. No, I'd stayed home; was feeling a bit under the weather that morning, you know. So it's really quite lucky that I just happened to be out walking Peony at that time in the afternoon! And how are you doing today, Miss? Are you feeling quite better?"

"I'm fine, Mr. Simmons. I actually have to head out the door now. Going back to school today," Margery rolled her eyes at her mom as she walked up to the phone, and Mr. Simmons continued to jabber on. Her mom had her work clothes on and a purse slung over her shoulder. This morning, she was holding two brown paper bags in her hand.

"Mr. Simmons?" her mom mouthed. Margery nodded. More loudly, Margery's mom said, "Okay, Marge! We've got to get going! You don't want to be late!"

"Oh, I see, Dear. Your Mum wants you out the door. Better not get in trouble, you know! Have a good day. I did so love studying when I went to school. I went to an even smaller school, you see, when I was—"

"Bye, Mr. Simmons!" With that, Margery put the receiver down (it's like your cell phone, but you know, bigger), and she and her mom walked out the door. After her mom locked the door, she handed her one of the paper bags.

Margery's heart sank, feeling the heft of the bag. There was at least a sandwich and an apple in there, she knew it. And as much as she said she knew she needed help, and really, she *did* know it, honest; she was still pretty scared of eating.

It might sound odd if you've never experienced it yourself: being scared of eating, that is. But remember, over the past few months Margery had convinced herself that Food was Bad. That eating would make her fat, and that fat would make her unlovable. Unworthy of attention. Ugly.

So, naturally, even though she knew she was unhealthy, starting to eat the foods that she had labeled "Bad" was going to be a really scary thing. She knew she needed to gain some weight back in order to be healthy, but she was scared to do it.

Now, I have a suspicion that you, too, have been a little scared of food at one time or another. You know what it's like to be scared to gain weight. Scared of not being able to control how much or what you eat. Scared of eating the wrong things.

That's totally okay—a ton of other kids and adults are often scared of eating too. So, don't sweat it. It takes time.

And I'm here to help.

———————

Margery's mom saw her looking inside her lunch bag, frowning, while she sat in the passenger seat of the car on the way to school. It was getting well into fall, and they were both bundled up in scarves, coats, and gloves while the old blue sedan's heater warmed up.

"Hey, you going to that group today after school?" Margery's mom asked, nervously. She didn't really know how to help, even though she saw her daughter was upset about the sandwich she'd packed. But she really was trying her best. (As a matter of fact, Cynthia had packed herself a sandwich for lunch that day rather than a salad, once she realized how much her own diet choices had affected her daughter's.)

"Yeah. I'm going."

Just a few minutes later, Margery hopped out of the barely warm car. She turned to close the door, and just before she did, smiled up at her mom, an unsaid thank you in her eyes. She slammed the door shut (you had to in this car) and jogged down the path and through the school's front doors as it had started to rain.

it's Like Chess Club... but Not.

After a rather uneventful day at school (okay, she got a B+ on a science quiz and accidentally dribbled some water down her shirt at the water fountain in front of Jax Davis, only like the cutest guy in her year), Margery went to her first meeting of SLBL. It was in a vacant math classroom in the 10th-year hall.

"Okay, everybody. Thanks for coming," the roundish boy with dark brown skin Margery had seen in the doorway of Ms. Steppin's room said. Next to him sat Ms. Steppin herself, pale as snow in comparison, and to her left, the ruddy school counselor whose name Margery thought was Becky Sherman. (It was Betty, actually.) In the other chairs in the circle were students.

Jordan

There were students from Margery's year all the way up until eleventh (American translation: eleven to sixteen years old). One of the girls in the group was very thin; so thin it hurt Margery's bones to look at her, like they might snap. Her brown, mousy hair was pulled back tightly on her head, and her cheekbones jutted out, feline-like. There was a girl who was heavy; round, with tightly curled black hair and dark skin. There was one blonde girl who looked, well, just fine. Not skinny, not heavy. Nothing that said to Margery she should be at a meeting called Self Love Body Love. And then there was Amanda Wallace—the most beautiful girl in the school, Margery thought.

Tabatha

Alexa

Jenny

Amanda

Then, all sitting together, just to the right of the group's apparent leader, were three other boys. One of them was also heavier—a redhead with a bland, friendly smile. One of them was very thin. The other was a boy with wavy, dark hair whose was covered in angry red splotches and pimples.

Patrick

James

J.P.

Margery observed all of this in a matter of seconds as she settled in.

"Well, today, we have two newbies to the club—Margery and Amanda. We'll go around and do introductions in a minute. First, though, I want to go over the mission here, because of Margery and Amanda."

Margery was both thrilled and embarrassed to be mentioned in the same breath as the most popular girl in school.

"Okay, so first off, this group is just for support. It's mostly focused on body image—but really, it's open to anyone who is struggling or knows someone who's struggling, basically with looks. Or confidence.

"So, just like chess club or math club or something, we meet in here every Monday and Wednesday after school. You don't have to come to all the meetings if you can't, but Mrs. Sherman recommends it." The boy gave a nod to Mrs. Sherman.

Mrs. Sherman

Margery was still glancing around the circle as he spoke, taking in everyone's appearance. She couldn't help it—her eyes were drawn to the skinniest girls, and then to Amanda. And she thought I shouldn't have eaten

- 44 -

that sandwich at lunch.

————————————

"... So that's basically what we do here at SLBL. Now, let's start with introductions for the newbs. Names, why you're here." The boy leaned back in his chair, hands behind his head, displaying his belly proudly. He had thick glasses perched on top of his mushroom-like nose, magnifying his almost black eyes. Margery had an urge to hug him.

"Alright then, I guess I'll start," Ms. Steppin said when nobody volunteered. "I want to add: this is a safe space — no one is in here who isn't, or hasn't been, struggling with, er... body stuff." No matter what she said, Margery thought, her voice sounded like music. Really, really, weird music.

WHAT IS THAT NOISE?

"My name is Karen Steppin, and I teach seventh year geography. I was bulimic as a teenager, which meant I threw up my food. I got help for it when I was twenty. It took a lot of hard work, but these days I consider myself healthy. And I even love my body, believe it or not. Well, most of the time." She started doing that very Ms. Steppin-like thing and trailed off in another direction completely, but then seemed to remember there was a room full of people looking at her. "Oh right. Well, I'm here to help in any way I can. So, that's that." She folded her hands in her lap.

Next to her, Mrs. Sherman smiled hugely. She was about sixty-years-old, Margery guessed,

(She was sixty-three, actually.)

And Margery had never seen her without a smile on her face. She thought it was weird.

(It was weird.)

"I'm Mrs. Sherman, and I'm here mostly to facilitate as a licensed therapist. But," at this her smile faltered, just a little, "I also struggle with my own body image. You know, getting older and all." She left it at that, and as she started smiling again, the fine wrinkles around her eyes and mouth pinched. The group's attention moved on to the next person: it was the thin, mousy-haired girl. She looked barely older than Margery.

"I'm Tabatha. I'm here because... well, I guess I'm anorexic. I started slowly cutting out foods about a year ago. Just trying to diet, you know. Lose a few pounds. But once I started I found it hard to stop. I kept cutting out foods. Soon I was starving. A month ago, I ended up in the hospital. I nearly died." Tears were swimming in Tabatha's eyes. If she blinked, they'd fall, but she was staring off far away, glassy-eyed.

"So I'm here for help. I need help to get healthy. To learn to like myself."

Margery marveled at her stick thin arms, her cheekbones that in a fashion magazine would have been "beautiful," but here in person, in real life, looked sort of scary. And then she realized something: this girl, this skinny, skinny girl, wasn't happy with her body. Not at all.

Around the circle it went—to the next girl, Alexa, with the dark, dark skin and black tightly curled hair. She said she struggled with eating too much; she couldn't control herself around sweets, especially when she was feeling sad or lonely. She'd started coming to the group two weeks ago, because she didn't know where else to turn. And so far, it was helping.

Next up was Margery. Margery being Margery, she tried to play it cool. Pretend that she was totally fine meeting a group of new faces—one of which was the most popular girl in school's. But I know she was quietly freaking out a little.

"I'm Margery and... well, I guess I'm here because I went to the hospital."

There was a pause.

"Do you feel like sharing why you needed to go to the hospital?" Ms. Steppin asked kindly, leaning forward.

"I fainted. I..."

At this, she faltered. She didn't want to admit it, but I gave her a little nudge.

"... I haven't been eating enough. And... well, I need help. I feel scared of food."

She thought everyone would laugh at her, but instead, most people in the group, nodded and said words of agreement. Margery felt a little less uncomfortable.

Next, the blonde girl, the one who Margery had labeled as "normal-looking," sat without speaking looking at her nails. When she finally looked up, she had tears silently streaming down her face. Margery immediately admired her bravery.

"I'm Jenny. I've been here a few times because, I hate that guys keep thinking they can look at me. Or whistle at me when I walk by. Or talk about my body. Or even put their hands on me. I've tried... like, telling them to stop. But then they just call me names. But, I mean, it's my body. So... that's why I've been coming here."

Margery noticed that the other older girls were all nodding in agreement, including Amanda Wallace. Up next, it was her turn.

"I'm Amanda," she said, "and I hate my body."

This is the part where Margery's brain did a little something like this:

"I feel like there's pressure on me, like, all the time to be pretty. Or skinny. Or not have zits. Or whatever. My sister is older and is, like, the perfect daughter. She moved to New York to go to school and models part-time, too. She's gorgeous, and she can, like, eat whatever she wants. And I feel all this pressure to be as pretty as she is—so I'm always watching what I eat. And comparing myself to other girls. And, I just feel like I'll never be good enough.

"So that's what I'm doing here." She looked around at everyone defiantly, her blue eyes shining and her golden hair an almost comically perfect cascade down her back.

Margery couldn't believe it: the prettiest girl in school—Amanda Wallace—hated her body?

Of course, you know by now that being beautiful

doesn't necessarily make you happier or make your life any better.

And fun fact—beauty is totally a matter of opinion. So while Margery thought Amanda was the bees knees (what? You guys don't say that??), someone else in the room may very well have thought she was.

Totally objective.

Anyway...

Onto the guys

Now, if you're a girl reading this, you might be thinking: What are guys doing in this meeting? Guys don't care about body stuff—they have it so easy!

Well, of course, if you're a guy reading this then you know that's total bogus. Guys deal with body stuff just like girls do—maybe in different ways, or maybe the same ways. But just know, this is something that can come up for boys, girls, and anyone in between.

Ahem.

"I'm J.P. I guess I'm just trying to gain some confidence here. Because, I don't have any. Like any. I'm sick of my face being so spotty and I'm sick of feeling like a loser to girls." At this, the boy named J.P., with dark brown hair, green eyes, and angry red spots covering his cheeks and forehead, glanced, timidly, to his right at Amanda, and then away. He nodded curtly to the guy next to him to go; Margery thought to get the attention off himself as fast as possible.

He was an Irish boy who looked about sixteen, with flaming red hair, light eyes, and round pink cheeks. His stomach was roundish, too, but he still seemed healthy, and as he talked, he rested his hands on top of it, contentedly.

"I'm Patrick. I've been coming to these meetings since the beginning two years ago. Then, I can't tell ya how shy I was. I couldn't talk to no one, let alone anyone I fancied. And no, I didn't lose any weight or anything, but I'm starting to get to a good place with how I feel about meself. It's hard to be fat and gay in school—but there ya are. That's me."

He smiled hugely at the rest of the group. Margery, again, felt a rush of admiration.

Next, the very thin boy, about two years older than Margery, told the room that he was tired of being picked on for being so scrawny. His dad (a total jock back in his day) was constantly on his back to join the football team, or run track, or do something! But James simply didn't like sports, and always wanted to tell his dad that just because he didn't play a sport didn't mean he wasn't doing something. But he was scared of him, and didn't.

Not even ping pong?!

15

And finally it was the group's leader, Jordan's turn. Margery looked at him again, closer this time, and noticed his dark, teddy bear-like eyes, his kind smile, the dimples that formed when he did. She hadn't even bothered to notice these things the first times she'd looked at him, because she'd been too stuck in her own head, worrying about herself.

"So, I'm Jordan," he said easily. His voice was loud and deep, clear as a bell. "I overeat whenever I'm upset—which lately, way things are going at home, is a lot. My parents are in the middle of a divorce," he added at everyone's raised eyebrows.

"But I've been coming to, and sometimes hosting, this group every Monday since school got in, so, yeah. Talking about it really seems to help." He smiled directly across the room at Margery, and as present as she was in that moment, she really felt it.

Of course, this didn't last long. As soon as she realized they were finished with the introductions, her thoughts started to race again.

What will we do next?

Will we have to work in groups?

Will I have to talk to Amanda?

What if I make an idiot of myself?

AaaAaaaAHHH!

"Okay, everyone!" Ms. Steppin called in her singsong voice. "We're going to try some CBT exercises today. Everyone will need a partner who's been here a few times, so they'll know how to guide it—" Margery breathed a sigh of relief. She wouldn't be with Amanda after all "—and one of you can partner up with me."

CbT

After a few minutes of negotiating chairs and moving around the room, Margery found herself sitting across from Jenny, the older girl who'd cried earlier. She immediately felt at ease with her for being so vulnerable and honest.

Each group was given a few pieces of paper with a table on it. The table was divided into several columns with things like "Situation" "Thoughts" and "Moods" labeled above each section. (Don't worry—there are a couple of these pages in the back for you.)

"Okay, girl," Jenny said, twirling a strand of blonde around her finger. She was about fifteen or sixteen and seemed to have taken Margery on as a sort of little sister. "You'll start by telling me about some sort of triggering event. By triggering event, I mean, like, something that made you do some sort of negative body image or food-related behavior. Like throw up, eat three pizzas, not eat at all, call yourself ugly, or you know, whatever your thing is."

Margery felt a little shocked at how relaxed this girl was being about everything. It seemed like she'd seen a lot.

"Okay..." Margery thought about what "her thing" was. She supposed it was just judging her body and being critical of herself, which led her to be scared of food. But she'd never really thought about there being a reason for that, other than her body itself. So she just thought of an event that she found stressful.

"Okay, I remember at the beginning of the school year. There was this boy. He was making fun of Mr. Pitts, and then I said something, and then he started making fun of me. He called me chubby. And... I guess that's about the time when all this started. This not eating. Being scared of food."

Jenny nodded once, sparing just a moment to give Margery a semi-sympathetic glance. "Right. So. What were you feeling in this situation?"

"Um, I guess I was sad. And mad. And maybe surprised. Just, like, really surprised that someone could say that. It was so embarrassing and hurtful."

"Which feeling is the 'hottest'? You know, like, which one thinking back on the event, do you feel the most?"

"Hurt."

"Okay, now tell me, what were your thoughts in the situation?"

"I thought he must be right. That I was fat. And when they laughed at me, I felt like no one would like me if I was fat, so I needed to get skinny."

Jenny glanced up from scribbling down these answers. Her lip was slightly puckered out, sad, and she looked for a moment younger than Margery.

"So you thought you were fat and that because of that no one would like you, right?"

Margery nodded.

"Okay. Now, can you give me some evidence that this thought is true?"

"Excuse me?" Margery said, surprised.

"I mean, like, what evidence is there that you were fat and because of that, no one liked you?"

Margery thought about it.

"Well, I mean, he said so. And, I mean, they laughed at me! Plus, I don't really have very many friends. I mean, there's Emma. But, I'm skinnier now so that's why she's probably my friend."

Even as Margery said it, she knew this wasn't true. Jenny seemed to know it too.

"You sure about that, kid? Were you and Emma only friends after you started losing weight?"

"Well, no. I guess we started hanging out before. And she said I was so funny..."

"Right. So, what evidence is there that the thought I'm fat and so no one will like me is not true?"

Yep. No evidence here.

Margery thought again. Immediately her brain filled up with a little list:

I wasn't fat in the first place.

Every time I went to the doctor, they always said I was in perfect health and didn't ever say I needed to lose weight.

Those boys were just trying to hurt my feelings by calling me chubby, because I called them out for being mean and embarrassed them.

And whether someone is "fat" or not is just a

description of their shape. Not an insult.

I do have friends.

I have friends that I made before I lost all this weight, like Emma and the other kids in Choir.

Tori was my best friend, and she never thought of me as fat. Or skinny. Or anything other than her best friend.

I miss Tori.

After she relayed this list of evidence to Jenny, Margery was surprised to find herself crying. She quickly wiped her tears away and looked around the room to make sure no one had noticed. But to her surprise, Jenny the Tough Girl, wrapped her in a hug and said "It's good to cry when you feel like crying."

And so Margery cried.

"I really miss my best friend, Tori," Margery finally said, wiping her nose on her sleeve. She didn't really realize how lonely she'd been since Tori had left.

"I bet your best friend not being around made you pretty lonely and really aware of whether or not people like you," Jenny noticed. Margery nodded.

"And I bet when those boys called you 'chubby,' you thought they must be right—and that's why you weren't making a lot of friends. Not because you just missed your friend, Tori."

Margery had never thought of it this way. She was blown away.

"You're right! And I remember after those guys made fun of me that one time, I felt really scared of food and scared of being fat every time I felt lonely or like I didn't have friends."

Margery thought back to all those times she felt lonely. How immediately, instead of feeling the loneliness, she would think about how she needed to lose weight, or she would even look at herself in the mirror and criticize her curves.

DON'T FEEL THE LONELINESS!

QUICK— LOOK OVER THERE!

EGO

"Right. So the last part of this exercise is to choose a different, more balanced thought, with both the evidence that yes that thought was true, and no it wasn't."

Margery thought. Then it hit her:

"Those boys were just trying to hurt my feelings by laughing at me for being chubby. But because I was lonely and scared of not having any friends, I thought they must be right, and that I needed to change. But really, I was just feeling lonely and insecure. It wasn't ever about my body at all!"

Margery could not believe it. This whole time she thought that she wanted to lose weight because of her body. She thought she was starving herself because of her body. Because she wanted to be skinny. She'd never realized that it was about the feelings underneath!

She and Jenny went back and forth with the CBT exercise for the next hour. Jenny was older and discussed things that Margery had only heard about— guys looking at her, whistling at her, calling her names, trying to touch her butt, and when she wouldn't let them, starting rumors about her.

Margery hoped that she wouldn't have to face stuff like this, but had a feeling she might.

After one exercise where Jenny had told her a story about some guy whistling at her in the hallway at school, and Jenny had gone home and cried, Margery asked:

"So what's a more balanced thought?"

Jenny had thought about it. And she came up with this:

"No one can tell me what my body is or isn't—whether it's pretty or ugly, or good, or bad. No one can tell me whether they can touch my body or not. Or whistle at it. Or even look at it. It's my body and it's my choice."

Here, here.

MY BODY, MY CHOICE.

After each exercise, Margery grew more and more certain about one thing: This body stuff—it's usually not about the body at all.

homework

That night when Margery got home from her meeting, she found that for the first time in a while she was excited to get to her homework. No, not Ms. Steppin's assignment on labelling all the states in the United States and their capital cities (for real— who needs to know this?), but the exercises she was given from her group meeting.

She rushed through dinner, hardly even noticing or caring that she was eating stuffed portabella mushrooms with rich, creamy sauce (something she'd have been quite aware of just a week ago.) After she cleared her plate, she kissed her mom on the cheek and bolted into her room. She poured the contents of her bag onto her bed and grabbed the little sheet of paper with her group assignments.

The first one was simple. Margery pulled out a separate piece of paper from her notebook, and with a thick purple marker wrote:

I LOVE AND ACCEPT MYSELF NO MATTER WHAT.

She then took the piece of paper to the bathroom and taped it to her mirror.

The second assignment took a bit more time and thought—she had to write a letter to her body about what it does for her and what she was thankful for. Then, to top it off, she had to write a letter from her body to herself about how it felt it had been treated by her and by the world. So she curled up on her bed and wrote and wrote by the light of her bedside lamp.

By the time she was finished, she had cried more than she'd cried in months. Maybe years. Maybe ever. She realized in writing the letters that she'd been treating her body pretty badly—and that the world was a pretty mean place to bodies too, sometimes.

brain food

The next day, Margery woke up at 6:43—before her alarm even went off. She laid in bed for several minutes just feeling her body; there was a curious bubbly sort of sensation in her stomach, and her eyes were wide open. Her head felt somehow open and clear.

It took her a moment to place it, but she realized she was actually feeling... good. Energized, awake, excited for the day, and for the first time in many mornings, her stomach felt properly hungry. Not empty and starving, but ready to eat.

"Morning, Marge," her mom said when she walked into the kitchen. She was wearing her favorite worn, light blue bathrobe and a pair of low, grey exercise socks. The shock of seeing her mom still in a bathrobe at this time of day was so distracting, Margery hardly even noticed what her mother was doing.

"Are you making... eggs?" Margery asked, standing in the doorway.

"I am indeed. And turkey sausage," her mom added, turning around. "I spoke to Janet this morning; I'm going to head into work at 8:30 rather than 7:30 this week so I can take you to school. Don't worry—it's not a big deal," she added, already knowing that Margery would protest. So instead, Margery just sat down at the table and waited for her breakfast.

Now, for the past several months, Margery had basically been living under the rule of "Food is Bad," so of course, her attitude wasn't going to change overnight. It would take time; she and her mom knew it would take time (as Mrs. Sherman told them both); but as she managed to finish most of the plate with fewer scary thoughts than she'd thought, she felt pretty proud of herself.

"Well, I don't think I've had such a satisfying breakfast in years," Cynthia said, clearing both their plates. That Margery didn't have to go through this alone meant more to her than she could say. So she didn't; she just hugged her mom, eggy plates in hand and all.

Meeting Number Two

That day and the next at school passed without much to do. She noticed that with enough food in her stomach, she was immediately more energized and could focus better in classes—which, fortunately for her meant getting an A+ on her geography test. (She did miss that whole Albany is the capital of New York thing, though, because seriously— why?)

She was beginning to spend more time with Emma again, here and there in between classes. Admittedly, it was still a bit awkward, as it tends to be after not talking to a friend for a while. And no, they weren't back to sitting together at lunch just yet; but still, by the time Margery's second meeting rolled around, she was feeling much better. Confident. Which is a good thing, because, let me tell you: it was a big one.

"Okay, everyone. Great to see you all," the very skinny

girl, Tabatha, was leading the group for today. Just like last time, everyone went around and said their names (Margery thought it might be because she and Amanda were still pretty new.)

(She was right)

And then Ms. Steppin instructed everyone to do something almost unheard of in school: Get comfortable and close their eyes.

"If that means laying down on the floor, that's okay, too. I brought some pillows. Just get comfortable."

Margery situated herself in her chair with a pillow behind her back and rested her hands on her knees.

"Now I want everyone to just keep your eyes closed. And breathe in and out slowly. Notice how the breath moves in through your nose—really feel it—and down, down, into your lungs and then your belly. Notice the pause at the bottom. Then notice how it flows up, up, and slowly exhales."

They did this over and over until Margery totally forgot about everything in the world but her breathing. There was no room. No people judging her. No self-judgment. She was just breathing, and for the first time in her life, totally present with her breathing.

And that, my friend, is what they call meditation.

After several minutes in silent meditation, Ms. Steppin said in a very soft voice, "Now notice the feelings in your body. Notice how your hands seem to tingle with energy. Notice this tingling all over your body. Notice if there is any tension, or discomfort. Notice the areas in your body where there is lots of space. What does it feel like to be in your body today? What does it feel like to be alive?"

Once again, Margery felt like her brain had just exploded, because never before had she sat still and just felt what it felt like to be in her body. She felt the tingling in her fingertips. The beat of her heart in her chest and even in her ears. She felt her strong muscles working to hold up her back and her head.

She'd never really felt her body before, from the inside. And it was freakin' awesome.

Sharing is Caring. and Crying. Lots of Crying.

After the meditation and noticing exercise, again, Ms. Steppin and Mrs. Sherman divided the group into pairs. This time, they were asked to discuss the "letter writing" assignment if they'd done it. They were welcome to read their letters to each other, but didn't have to, and were encouraged to share their feelings about the exercise with each other.

Now, this time around, Margery was paired with J.P.— the boy who was self-conscious about his skin being spotty and not getting attention from girls. Margery felt a little embarrassed about reading her letter out loud to a boy, after all, what would he understand about body image?

But to her surprise, J.P. unashamedly offered to read

his letters to her first. And as he read, she was surprised to find that his words may as well have been her own.

"Dear body,

"I know I haven't been so nice to you lately. I know I've been blaming a lot of stuff on you, body. But really, when I think about it, I know you're a good body. You are strong and healthy—and a lot of people aren't so lucky. You let me run fast—which I love to do. You let me climb trees. You let me play with our dogs. You get me where I need to go, and you even keep me from getting sick.

"I, like, never get sick," he added to Margery, flipping the paper over. "It's weird."

On the other side was his letter from his body to himself.

"Dear J.P.," he cleared his throat and blinked; Margery saw that his eyes were wet.

"It's your body here. I know that you feel grateful for all the things I do for you. But like you said, you've been blaming a bunch of stuff on me. And it sucks.

"I'm just your body, man. I'm doing my best just to keep you healthy and safe—and yeah, you have acne. But you're thirteen. Lots of other people have acne. I feel like you ~~Yeah. We pretty much all have acne.~~ take everything out on me. When you feel lonely, when you feel shy or embarrassed around girls you like, or when you're stressed out. You always attack me—you look in the mirror and tell your reflection how ugly you are. It hurts.

"I'm tired of being hurt by you, and everyone else who judges me just for what I look like. People who

- 63 -

laugh at me because there's a little acne. I'm tired of the world saying that everything has to look a certain way—because I think we all know that's stupid. Everyone looks different. I'm just doing my best here.

"I hope you'll stop being so mean to me.

"Love,

"Your Body"

In the short time that it took J.P. to read his letter, Margery felt closer to him than she did to some people she'd known for years. She hastily wiped away the wetness from her eyes and awkwardly reached out a hand, as though to put it on his. As though to say I know just how that feels, or Don't worry, you're not alone. But the words wouldn't come, so, instead, she just handed him her own letters to read.

They went a little something like this:

Dear Margery,

It's your body. It's hard for me to write right now because I am crying and my hands are shaking. But you know that, you're here too, aren't you?

Anyway. I'm hurt. And I'm unhealthy. And all I've tried to do is stick around and keep you safe and happy. But lately you've been pretty hard on me. You've been constantly comparing me to other bodies. You've been telling me I can't eat what I want to. Then if I do, you get mad at me, or even make me throw up.

I know you think it's because the world is putting a lot of pressure on you to look a certain way. And that's true too. Magazines and shows and images are everywhere of skinny women looking a certain way. And girls like you think you're supposed to look like those images—which you learned last night weren't always even real!

(She had: Margery had done some investigating and learned that almost all of those glossy magazine photos of women were heavily edited and Photoshopped.)

But Margery, more than anyone else: you're putting pressure on me. And you do it when you feel stressed out, or sad, or lonely. It's not about me, Margery. I'm just your body. I'm your friend. And I'm here for you.

Next time you're feeling sad, feel the sadness. But don't take it out on me.

Love,

Your Body

———————

Dear Body,

I know I'm supposed to thank you, but first, I have to say: I'm sorry. I've been treating you so badly lately. I look in the mirror at you and think how much better you could and should be. I talk to you in ways I would NEVER talk to a friend.

So I'm sorry. I know you're just trying to keep me healthy and safe. And thank you. Thank you for letting me be strong enough to run and play. Thank you for letting me have a voice to sing in Choir. For letting me laugh and feel joy. For letting me cry. For letting me really feel what it is to be alive.

Everything I do in life is through you, Body. You're my best friend. And I'm going to try to treat you better from now on—I promise.

I love you so much,
Margery

Spaghetti Squash and Sentence Stems

How I feel about my body is...

How I think others see me is...

How I feel about food is...

When Margery's mom picked her up after the meeting, Margery's face was still red and puffy from crying. Now, like I mentioned pretty early on, Cynthia was not exactly the warmest and cuddliest and most emotionally available of moms. She was tough. But as you've seen, as Margery was opening up and growing up, so was her mom. (FYI: You never stop growing up.)

"What's wrong? Were you crying?" she asked as soon as Margery climbed into the little sedan. It was cold enough outside that the heat was fogging up the windows, even though the defroster was on. But at least it was warm.

"I'm fine. I'm... good, actually," Margery said, realizing that in fact, she hadn't felt so good in a long time. After a few moments of silence, Margery told her mom about the letters, to which Cynthia smiled.

"I'm proud of you, Marge. You're doing some hard work, you know. It's brave."

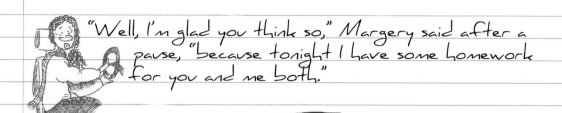

"Well, I'm glad you think so," Margery said after a pause, "because tonight I have some homework for you and me both."

———

After a delicious meal of spaghetti squash with pesto and mozzarella balls, sundried tomatoes, and chicken, Margery and her mom sat down for dessert. It was the first "treat" she'd allowed herself in months, and perhaps the first "treat" her mom had had in years. She had forgotten how much she loved coconut ice cream; and Cynthia literally licked her bowl clean.

It was during their second serving that Margery decided to bring out the homework:

Some sentence stems.

She passed the sheet of paper over to her mom, and her mom peered over it, holding her spoon in her mouth.

"Oof! Whatever happened to bringing home math homework?" she joked. Margery could see she was a bit nervous, but she moved aside her nearly finished bowl of ice cream and placed the paper down in front of her. "Okay, let's do it."

The homework exercise was a sheet of sentence stems that both she and Margery would do, out loud, together. Don't worry, you'll have these same sheets in the back of the book. They're fun—plus, you might even learn a few of your parent's secrets. And that's always nice.

"How I feel about my body is... blank," her mom read aloud.

She was nervous, Margery could tell. This was a stretch for her mom, who was about as open emotionally as a rock.

SENTENCE STEMS

"Okay, how I feel about my body is... it's really strong. And I'm... afraid of it getting older. And saggy. And... I've always feared gaining weight or not being able to exercise. Even when I was young."

At this, Cynthia looked at Margery, guilt-stricken, for it was then that she realized how much her own obsession with weight had rubbed off on her daughter.

Margery just nodded and repeated the exercise for herself. "How I feel about my body is... I sometimes feel trapped inside of it. And, like, no matter what I do, or how skinny I get, it's never good enough. I feel like my body would be happier if I just stopped worrying about everything."

Cynthia smiled sadly, for the first time seeing just how grown up her daughter was suddenly becoming, and then moved on to the next prompt before she could cry.

"I think others see my body as... well, I don't know. Pretty good for my age, I suppose." Cynthia held out an arm, examining it. To Margery, her mom's dark, smooth, brown skin was perfect. Even with the wrinkles here and there. "I think others see my body as... well, just a body. Now that I think about it, I bet other people don't notice my body nearly as much as I do."

"Yeah, I think others see my body as... too skinny,

unhealthy, if they notice," Margery replied. "But now that you mention it, I think people aren't paying as much attention as I thought they were. I'm the hardest on myself out of everyone."

That, my friends, is what they call an "aha" moment.

AHA!

After a few more sentence stems— What I think you think about me is... What I think about me is... Something I wish more people knew about me is... One of the best experiences I've ever had in my body was... Margery and her mom were finished. They'd moved from the kitchen into the living room several rounds ago, and were sitting, exhausted, on either end of the couch.

"I had no idea you wished more people knew your feminine side," Margery side, remembering her mom's words. She'd always thought of her mom as so tough—as both her mom and her dad. She never would have guessed she even had a feminine side.

"Yes, well. I'm sure if they did I wouldn't be going out with so many—well. It would just be nice to meet a real man for a change. Someone with his act together."

Margery nodded, only half knowing what her mom was talking about.

"Anyway, that was... good, kiddo. I'm not usually very open with my emotions, but I think that was good. Exhausting, but good." She got up and kissed her daughter on the forehead, something she hadn't done in what seemed like years, grabbed her water glass, and headed down the hall to her room.

Margery went to her room and finished up the rest of her school homework, and finally, at nearly midnight, went into the bathroom to brush her teeth. Her face was puffy, red, and the little mascara she wore was stained down her cheeks. Her nose was snotty. She was beat. She was still too thin—or too fat—or too short—or just not quite good enough—

And then she caught sight of the little note on the edge of her mirror:

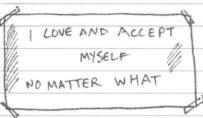

> I LOVE AND ACCEPT
> MYSELF
> NO MATTER WHAT

And for just a moment, all those critical thoughts vanished, and she really felt it. She was enough. She'd always been enough. Would always be good enough. No matter what.

Oh Yeah, You're Funny

The next morning at school, Margery noticed that there was still a small part of her brain worried about someone running up to her, shouting something like: Oh, em gee! You're so not skinny anymore. What happened to you?! But as nobody seemed to be paying her or her body the slightest attention, she started to think maybe she was right: she really was the center of her own world.

OH.
EM.
GEE.

And when nobody had come by to drive-by insult her 20 minutes after she got there, she was feeling reassured. With a sigh of relief, she grabbed her books and headed to first period.

Okay, to be clear, just because she was feeling good and confident doesn't mean that math was any less boring for her—especially since they had one Ronald Daniels substituting. Now, I'm the all-loving, totally blissed out, accepting, peaceful, universal Is, so I know nothing of judgment or negativity—

But I'll tell you this: A mop would have been a more interesting teacher than Mr. Daniels. He simply lacked that— what's it called? Charisma? Charm?

PROFESSOR JONES

Uh...

Personality?

So Margery decided to liven things up a bit.

Mr. Daniels stood up front—a tall and thin and rather unremarkable looking middle-aged man. He had a forgettable face and rather dull muddy-colored hair. His voice even seemed to come out of his mouth slowly, all the while his eyes drooped sleepily. It was like his own face was bored of his voice.

I am not a mop.

Every time he called on her with that long, drawn out tone, she'd answer him politely, and then, stand up and bow to the entire class. They'd clap appreciatively and laugh. Encouraged, she started singing the answers back to him. They ate it up. In the end, after answering a particularly difficult question by rapping (with the accompanying beat box of Trevor Phillips), the class roared in applause and she ran down the aisle of desks giving high fives.

"Oh yeah - you're funny, bruh!" the shaggy-haired Dan

Belvridge remarked from the sit behind her, as though just remembering. She was funny. And she'd forgotten, too.

Love and Mashed Potatoes

Margery, Mrs. Sherman, and Cynthia had all decided it best for Margery to bring her own lunches to school until she felt totally comfortable with not dieting—which, as Mrs. Sherman pointed out, could take a while. When she walked into the cafeteria, the center was total empty, as most other people were just getting into line. So she had her choice of tables. A little cautiously, she walked over to the usual Choir Table. She hadn't sat there in what felt like forever, because for a while she was skipping lunch altogether and didn't want anyone to know.

She was nervous.

She pulled out her tuna sandwich on whole wheat bread. Her apple and almond butter. A little side of carrots. A bottle of coconut water. She stared at it, all the while her stomach in knots.

Then, just as she was about to finally take a bite of her sandwich, she heard his voice call from behind her:

"Hey—Margery, right?"

It was mousy boy. Connor.

She put her sandwich down, sure he'd come over to tell her to stop eating, that she was getting fat again. But all he said was, "My friend James said you actually managed to make Mr. Daniels' class fun today. Mind coming by our class with him after lunch? I got an F on my science test. I could use a laugh."

She was spared doing anything but looking surprised, as just then a crowd of people from the lunch line walked over, and one of them punched Connor in the shoulder and they started laughing.

"Boys are so stupid," a voice said from across the table. Margery looked over and saw Emma—all wrapped up in a puffy coat, scarf, and fluffy hat, carrying her lunch tray. Not to anyone's surprise, it was piled high with mashed potatoes. Just... mashed potatoes.

"Want to go sit outside?" she asked.

Margery nodded, pulled on her own coat and hat, and gathered her lunch to head out the double doors.

"So I've been really worried about you," Emma finally said as they sat down on a bench outside. It really was getting too cold for this, but it was one of the last sunny days, so they tried to pretend they weren't freezing. "I was trying to find a good way to say it, but I don't think there really is one."

Margery nodded. She was finding it hard to chew her sandwich. There was a lump in her throat. Thankfully, Emma kept talking.

"I mean, I know I can't really understand it all. But I've been talking to Mrs. Sherman a lot about all of it lately, and, I just want you to know that I'm here for you, no matter what, and—"

"You've been talking to Mrs. Sherman lately, because you've been worried about me?" Margery said, finding her voice.

"Well, yeah!"

Margery couldn't help it, she was so touched at her friend's concern and love for her, she burst out crying. So did Emma. The two were hugging and crying and crushing Emma's tray of potatoes and cold and snotting and—

And none of it mattered, because in that moment, Margery felt more loved and cared for than she knew she could.

Slumber Party

The weekend came in a rush of wind and dark, heavy, thunderclouds. By the time Emma arrived at Margery's for their sleepover, the rain was coming down so violently, umbrellas were all but useless, and both Emma and her mom looked as though they'd swum to the house.

"So sorry to burst in on you like this!" Emma's mom said. "I'm Elizabeth, but you can call me Liz." She stuck out her hand to shake Margery's just as Cynthia was rounding the corner into the little home's entryway.

"Oh hello. You must be Emma's mum," she said, wiping her hand on her pants. She'd been baking something in the kitchen and had a dusting of powdered sugar and flour on her hands.

"Yes, I'm Liz. It's good to finally meet you! I was going to just drop Emma off, but I'm having a bit of car trouble. Mind if I use your phone*?"

Cynthia, of course, said yes (I mean, how weird would it have been if she said "no," right?) and guided Liz into the kitchen.

*Yes, if you can believe it, this was before everyone had a cell phone.

"C'mon," Margery said to Emma. "You should change into some dry clothes or you'll get sick."

So the two girls went down the short hall, through the living room where a warm fire was blazing, and into Margery's room. Emma changed into some flannel pajamas she'd brought over, and Margery slipped on her favorite, coziest, and ugliest slippers. When she turned around she saw Emma looking at something on her desk.

"Oh—that's just some of the, uh, homework. From the group I've been going to."

Emma did one of those "May I?" motions and with Margery's nod of approval, she picked up a piece of paper and started reading. It was an exercise Margery hadn't actually done yet:

Directions: Each person should choose an object in the room, and for 12 minutes, notice and appreciate everything about it, verbally or nonverbally. Then close your eyes and notice and appreciate the feeling of appreciation. Then in partners, choose another object, and appreciate it together for 23 minutes. Finally, each person will take turns telling their partner what they notice and appreciate about him or her. End with a short meditation for participants to appreciate the feeling of appreciation in themselves.

"It sounds lame, I know," Margery said before Emma could say anything at all. She felt embarrassed that her friend, who she thought was so perfect, read something so personal. Something that made it clear Margery needed help. And clearly, Emma did not. "Let's go pick out a movie," Margery added hastily as Emma opened her mouth to say something.

So she put down the paper and the two made their way, slippers padding quietly along the wood floors, into the living room. There, their moms were sitting on the couch, laughing loudly together like old friends. On the coffee table in front of them was a veritable feast of snacks—a giant bowl of rainbow caramel popcorn, a square tray dotted with seed crackers, apple slices, and little cubes of cheese, an open box of pizza simply spilling over with vegetables, carrots and dip, chips and salsa, and even, to Margery's delight and horror, a small plate of freshly baked and still gooey chocolate chip cookies.

"What's all this?" she asked, stepping into the room.

"Oh, well, it's for the slumber party!" Margery's mom announced brightly. "I don't know if you guys have been paying attention, but look—"

She gestured at the T.V. which was tuned to the news.

On it was a map of England, and just over their small town, was a giant splotch of color dotted with raindrops and hail.

"My car broke down outside, so I was going to have dad come pick me up," Liz said to Emma, gesturing for the girls to come join them. "But then the storm turned from bad to, well, this—" she pointed at the T.V., "so I hope you don't mind, but it looks like I'll be sleeping here tonight."

"Cool!" said Emma. In two long-legged strides, she was at the coffee table, and a moment later, sitting on the floor next to it, helping herself to a piece of pizza dipped in the carrots' ranch dressing.

Margery smiled and walked into the room too. It was so warm and inviting, but she was feeling... something. Something was off, and she couldn't quite put her finger on it.

triggering

But, of course, I could.

Margery was feeling uncomfortable being around so much food that to her was "triggering." Triggering here just means that it made her emotions jump like a scared cat. She was really emotionally vulnerable—and reactive. She was

WHAT THE — also always a bit uncomfortable meeting new adults—it made her feel like an outsider, or like she didn't know quite how to behave to fit in. Or if she was supposed to fit in. Or what.

So to her, she knew something was up... but she wasn't quite sure what. So instead of observing the feelings, or talking to someone about them, or even excusing herself to go into her room and take a few breaths—she did something that probably a lot of you have done, too:

She ate.

It was hard for Margery, because Emma was sitting next to her—her stick-thin friend who was always hungry. And it seemed her mom, Liz, was much the same way. The two just ate and ate. They ate throughout the movie. (They chose *Big*.) They ate as they talked after the movie (about guys at school, men Cynthia was dating, and just briefly, and with a lot of protest from Emma, Emma's dad.)

So Margery did, too. Not because she was hungry, but because she felt uncomfortable. And the more she ate, the number she felt to her emotions.
Until it was over. And she panicked.

People were separating—her mom was starting to clear the dishes. "Wow—we ate almost all of the food! I'm impressed," she remarked lightly from the kitchen. Liz was on the phone, twirling the cord between her fingers as she talked, and Emma was waiting for Margery on the edge of the room, yawning widely, ready to get some sleep.

But Margery hardly noticed any of this, because in her mind it was as though someone had hit the panic button:

CAN'T BELIEVE YOU ATE ALL THAT!

YOU'RE GOING TO GET FAT!

YOU WORKED SO HARD!

YOU THREW IT ALL AWAY!

COOKIES + PIZZA!

PANIC

Of course in that moment, everything she learned from her group about staying present, about mindfulness, about self-compassion—all of it went flying right out the window.

"Yeah, I'll be right there," Margery mumbled. She made her way straight to the bathroom in the hall, and got down on her knees next to the toilet. Panicked, she tried to make herself throw up.

And it wouldn't work.

She tried again.

It still wouldn't work.

At this point she was crying, her throat hurt, and she felt totally and utterly helpless. She did her best to wipe up her eyes, still feeling intensely guilty about the food she'd eaten, and got to her feet, left the bathroom, and joined Emma in her room.

appreciation yo

"Oh my god, what's wrong?" was the first thing Emma said when she came in. Okay, so apparently she hadn't done that great a job wiping away the tears.

Margery's mind was racing, trying to find some excuse for crying, some lie. Anything.

But then, just for a moment, she remembered. She stood there, closed her eyes, and just breathed. She breathed in deeply, noticing each detail of the breath, and then breathed it out. And in that brief moment, she could honestly feel her emotions for the first time that night.

"I can't stand myself sometimes," she said quietly. She walked over to her bed and sat on it hard, burying her face I her hands. "I just ate so much food—and then I felt really guilty about it and I tried to make myself throw up. And it didn't work. And even if it had, I would have felt so guilty about that. And, you know, I don't expect you to understand because you're, like, perfect."

At this Emma made a sound of utter disbelief.

"What?"

"I am not perfect. Are you crazy? I'm far from perfect. I'm failing three classes right now, and my dad says if I don't start doing better, I'll end up getting held back or something. Only, you know, he's an accountant so he uses math all the time. He loves it." Emma walked over to the desk and pulled out the little wooden chair. She sat down on it and sighed.

"Hey."

Margery looked over to where Emma was sitting. She was looking down at the SLBL group homework.

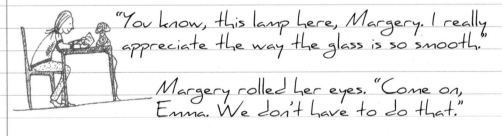

"You know, this lamp here, Margery. I really appreciate the way the glass is so smooth."

Margery rolled her eyes. "Come on, Emma. We don't have to do that."

"No seriously. I really like this lamp; I've just ever mentioned it before. The glass is perfectly smooth."

She was looking at the lamp on Margery's desk—a

blown glass lamp, with a glass base and shade, all swirling reds and oranges. When it was on, it looked like fire. Emma was doing the appreciation exercise.

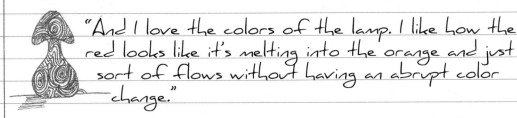

"And I love the colors of the lamp. I like how the red looks like it's melting into the orange and just sort of flows without having an abrupt color change."

Margery got up and walked over to stand near the desk.

Here's what was going on inside Margery:

This is so stupid. What good does it do to appreciate some lamp? I feel embarrassed. This is not cool at all. What would the other kids think if they knew this is how Emma and I were spending our Friday night?

But then she remembered something that Ms. Steppin had said about the importance of being vulnerable. And she said:

"I like the way the lamp looks like it's made out of fire, or lava, when it's on. It makes the walls and desk glow red."

And back and forth the two went, appreciating the lamp. Margery had never realized how many things she could find to appreciate about the simple thing (32, to be precise!), and when they were done, they chose another object: a blue vase on Margery's windowsill.

They remarked on its shape, color, the light bouncing off of it; even the shadow it cast. They were so busy appreciating, and fully noticing this object for the first time, Margery completely forgot about how miserable she had felt.

And then they moved on to the next part of the exercise: appreciating each other.

Margery felt nervous all the sudden. The wheels in her head started spinning again almost immediately, telling her that it would be hard for Emma to think of anything; that she should just call the game to an end; that there was nothing worth noting about her.

But just then, Emma launched into not just one appreciation, but a whole list of them. By the time she'd reached number five, Margery sat down on the floor, leaning her back against her bed.

"You are one of the funniest people I've ever met.

"You're so strong. You've been through a lot, and you're working your way through it.

"You're brave.

"You're vulnerable.

"You value growth.

"You care so much about other people.

"Your hair is, like, the best in our year.

"I wish I had your dark skin.

"You hardly ever get zits—I get them all the time.

"You're charismatic. All the teachers love you.

"You're super smart.

"You became my friend when I was really lonely. I don't know if you knew that, but I was really down at the beginning of the year, after my sister went off to school.

"I appreciate the way your eyelashes curl up.

"I appreciate your pants. (Where did you get those?)

"I appreciate you doing this group—that takes a lot of guts."

And on and on it went for a whopping 55 appreciations and observations. When Emma was finished, Margery gave her a big bear hug in gratitude. Then, Emma refused to let Margery give her appreciations—"Not tonight," she said, "tonight, just let these things sink in. Sometime soon I'll need a list of appreciations, and then I'll know who to ask."

Soon after, the girls pulled the spare bed from beneath Margery's and within minutes of lying down, were fast asleep.

You gotta be kidding me

The rest of the weekend went by in a blur of rain, puddles, hail, sleet, and then eventually—and excitingly—snow. For about an hour.

By Monday, the storm had passed through and Margery's little town was left cold and with a few fewer leaves and branches from the violent winds, but just fine otherwise. If not a little grumpy about still having to go to school.

Margery was somewhat surprised to find that it was already the week before final exams for the semester (my how time flies when you're dealing with a personal emotional crisis), and was even more surprised when, after school, she discovered that it was the last group meeting until the New Year.

"You gotta be kidding me!" she said, causing all heads in the room to turn. Today's group was most of the usual suspects: Jordan, Ms. Steppin, Mrs. Sherman, Alexa, Tabatha, J.P., Patrick, James, and Amanda. Jenny had left town for holiday early.

"Well, no, unfortunately, dear, we're not kidding you. Next week you'll all be busy with your exams; you won't want to have meetings then. And over the holidays, the school will be closed. And besides, I'm going to the Canary Islands."

Mrs. Sherman allowed herself one of her actual genuine smiles just then; you could tell because it took up a little less of her face.

The thought of ending meetings altogether for almost a month seemed out of the question for Margery. Admittedly, she was nervous about them at first, but she found that more than anything, just talking to others in this group setting was helping her feel more comfortable with her body and with food. She didn't feel ready to be on her own again.

And then she realized, she didn't have to be.

"Well, I don't care. We can just meet at my house. My mom won't mind. I don't know about any of you guys, but I need support, especially during the holidays when my mom goes, like, berserk, putting the tree up and all."

WHICH ONE IS OUT? WHYYYY?!

There were nods of agreement. J.P. muttered something about his dad and the "Christmas lights fiasco."

A couple of people would be out of town for the holidays, but everyone else was excited about the meetings continuing over the break. Even Ms. Steppin said she'd be happy to lead them, since Mrs. Sherman would be leaving town. So, with that decided, Tabatha (who was taking a turn leading that day) launched into the instructions for their first exercise.

"Okay, everyone. We're going to partner you up with someone." Ms. Steppin walked around the circle, counting them off from one to four, like a game of Duck, Duck, Goose. The eight students held up their numbers and scanned the circle for their match.

Margery was a three. And so was Amanda.

Now, I tried to tell Margery to be cool—that it was okay. Amanda was just a girl, like Margery, even if she was considered to be popular. There was nothing to fear. Believe me, I was there the whole time just chillin'.

BE COOL, MAN!

But she was nervous.

"Hi, Amanda. I'm Margery. I guess you knew that already. Because of the group. Not because of school or anything, because we're not even in the same year. Maybe you didn't know that. If you didn't, I'm Margery."

Oh, my god, I'm such a nerd, she thought. She sat silently with her arms folded, vowing never to speak again, while Tabatha continued with the instructions.

"Okay, so, whoever's older in your pair will be 'A.' The other will be 'B.'"

Amanda nodded once, listening. Margery wondered if she'd remembered to put on deodorant that morning.

"Now As, I want you to imagine how you must seem to Bs. If you were looking at your own face in this moment—your words, your movements—how would it look from the outside? How would B feel about them? You can use the words 'I must seem' or 'I must look' to help you get started. We'll do this for two minutes, then switch. And go."

The room immediately filled with voices. Margery reluctantly looked over to Amanda, trying somehow to convey that she was cool and not nervous or uncomfortable, not at all; so she was surprised to see that Amanda looked downright terrified.

"I'm not good at this sort of thing," she said in a hushed voice, hard to hear over the rest of the room. After a moment she cleared her throat and began.

"I must seem... totally insecure to you. I must seem... like I care what other people think about me. Like, way too much. I must seem really shallow. I must seem stupid. Boring. I must seem scared. I must seem like a pushover. I must seem like an airhead. I must look like I spent an hour in front of the mirror today. I must look like I've gained weight since the beginning of the year. I must look bad, because my highlights are all grown out and I have these zits on my chin. I must seem totally vain to even care about this stuff. I must seem like a loser..."

And on and on she went. Amanda Wallace: the prettiest and most popular girl in school. She had the same insecurities and vulnerabilities as Margery. As anyone.

When her two minutes ended, she tucked her blond hair behind her ears shyly and looked over at Margery. It seemed like she was waiting for ridicule. Before Margery could say any words of comfort, or even crack a joke to break the tension, Tabatha was telling the room that it was now B's turn.

"I must seem... nervous," Margery started out cautiously. She had a story that she was bad at being vulnerable with her feelings.

But then she remembered how important vulnerability was. How Ms. Steppin had said that's "where the magic is." So she dug deeper.

VULNERABILITY

"I must seem like a nerd, because I don't have as many friends as you. I must seem really lame, because I'm nervous being around someone more popular than I am. I must seem ugly, because I don't look anything like you. I must seem like I'm trying too hard. I must seem young. Like a kid. I must look embarrassed. I must look fatter than I did when we started these meetings. I must seem unconfident."

Her two minutes were up.

Tabatha directed the group to sit in silence for a moment,

just looking at their partners. Which, at first would have been totally weird to Margery, but after just unloading all of that, it didn't seem that uncomfortable. She felt emotionally open. Vulnerable. Magic.

"Now you're going to take a couple of minutes and just share back with your partner how they do seem to you. You can tell them when you felt the most connected to them while they were talking. Whatever you'd like. These are open share backs."

This time, the room stayed quiet for a moment. Clearly everyone was feeling a little embarrassed about this part of the exercise. But once Patrick's deep voice filled the space, ("You're freakin' awesome, man!" Said to Jordan), everyone started talking again, albeit nervously.

Margery shared that Amanda, to her, seemed perfect. She blushed furiously when she said it, but it was the truth. And then it was too late to turn back, so she went on to tell her, "You're like the most popular girl in school, and I have no idea why you would think that you're not pretty enough, because every guy and some of the girls are totally in love with you." She went on to reveal that she'd read Amanda as confident and strong most of the time in school, but was surprised and impressed that she'd opened up about her insecurities in the group. The two minutes went by quicker than she'd expected. Then it was Amanda's turn.

"You seem so much healthier than you did when these meetings first started. You look so much better. You seem happier. You're clearly very smart and funny. And you strike me as strong for coming here and getting help at such a young age. For addressing a problem before it can become an even bigger problem. For sharing your story and your words and your jokes with all of us.

"You seemed scared when you first started the meetings, but you seem so much more confident now. You don't seem like a kid to me—you seem older. Maybe even older than I am. I admire your courage and your wit. You totally seem like someone I'd hang out with."

When the two minutes were finished, they were instructed to sit in silence and just let it all sink in. Margery could hardly believe it. She really felt the things Amanda had said. She felt brave, and strong, and funny. She felt more confident and grateful than she had in months.

CUPCAKES!

After that, the group spent some time talking about how that exercise made them feel. And then, to everyone's mixed excitement and horror, Ms. Steppin reached behind her chair and presented a light pink box filled with cupcakes.

"Okay, okay, calm down," for everyone was talking at once. After all, this was a group of people who were mostly somewhat scared of gaining weight or had body image issues, and Ms. Steppin here had just brought in a box of cupcakes.

"I'm going to pass the box around and everyone will take a cupcake. Don't worry—I baked them and they're allergy-free. Wait for everyone to get their cupcake."

She passed around the box. Margery felt uncomfortable

and when she looked at Tabatha across the circle—her thin, thin arms, her jagged cheekbones poking out of her face—she looked terrified. Margery guessed she hadn't allowed herself a cupcake in years.

"Now, just notice the cupcake, like you did in the noticing homework. Notice how it looks. How it smells. How it feels in your hand. If you'd like to, take a bite."

Margery's mouth was watering as she looked at the little chocolate cupcake. It was topped with a thick layer of pink cream frosting, and in the middle in red and white icing, was a somewhat messy candy cane.

"Chew it several times and really notice how it tastes. Notice how sweet it is. How it feels in your mouth. The texture of it. You can close your eyes if it helps," she added.

Margery did. She focused all her attention on chewing and tasting and really fully being present in eating that cupcake. And let me tell you—it was the best cupcake she'd ever had.

By the time she was halfway through with it, she found that she didn't even want the rest; just paying attention to the first half was enough.

Several of the other students had similar experiences, and they put their half-finished cupcakes back in the box.

"Eating mindfully is a great way to let your body talk to you. When you pay attention while you eat, your body will tell you when it's had enough. Plus, you'll just get to enjoy it more," Ms. Steppin added, licking a bit of frosting from her thumb.

Now it's time to Cry-a Lot

The final exercise for the day might as well have been called "Now it's time to cry a lot."

Because it was the last meeting (at least at school and with everyone) for a while, they went around the entire group, and focused on one person at a time, giving appreciations.

They all told Patrick how much they appreciated his bravery to just love himself and be himself; they told him how they appreciated his booming laugh and kindness. They told Amanda how they appreciated her opening up— sharing the story about her sister and her parents. They all laughed when they remembered how much they appreciated Tabatha's comment on the whole political debacle that had just happened. J.P. was told over and over again how much everyone appreciated his desire to be more vulnerable. Jordan: his charisma and confidence, even in the face of his parents' divorce and body struggles. Alexa: her mind-blowing insights and almost poetically beautiful words. James: his bravery in standing up to his father once and for all and starting to embrace his self-proclaimed "scrawny bod." And Margery, her sense of humor. Her ability to light up the room. To be brave. To share. To show up (as it turned out, she was the youngest in the room, which apparently gained her a lot of cred with the group), and of course, being committed enough to offer up her home for meetings over break.

The meeting closed with a giant group hug, with Margery smooshed, happier than she'd ever been, in the middle.

happy general holiday season!

Here's the part in the story where I make an executive decision, and speed things up a bit. Because, yes, Margery had a full week left in school, then final exams, and then several days of milling about her house doing things like cleaning her bookshelf and watching television. And sure, there were some good days and bad days, some sad days and mad days. But mostly, Margery was doing pretty well.

They'd had two meetings so far at her house—one at the beginning of their week of exams (which only J.P., Tabatha, and Jordan showed up for), and the next, the first Monday once break started.

They'd hang out in the living room—a far more casual setting than the rather sterile classroom with its hard, blue plastic chairs. They lounged, they talked more casually and more openly. They just hung out. It was nice. It felt like family.

When Margery's mom came home from work she was thrilled to have a house-full of kids. Ever the hostess, she insisted they all stay for dinner and a movie, and before they all left, she'd invited them over for a little party the following week for Christmas Eve Eve.

And so that, my dear friend, is where we will pick up. Because as much fun as hanging around the house while it snowed relentlessly outside was, and as thrilling as it would be to tell you all about how Margery and Emma had started putting together puzzles in the afternoons, the Christmas Eve

So...what is it?

Eve celebration was something to truly remember.

"Merry Christmas, Happy Chanukah, Happy Thursday, Merry Friday Eve. You know, Happy General and totally Secular Holiday Season of your choice!" Jordan announced as the door to Margery's opened for the fifth time that night.

Jordan was the first to arrive, because his dad had to drop him off on the way to his father-in-law's retirement home. He explained all of this, ducking his head into the hallway for a moment, as the wind howled and blew little flurries of snow in through the door.

After Jordan got there, Emma and her mom arrived. Liz and Cynthia had become fast friends the night of the slumber party. Almost as soon as they arrived, Emma explained somewhat self-consciously that her dad couldn't join them, because he was picking up her sister from the airport.

Next came J.P. with a girl he was dating (Margery gave him a not-so-discrete high five), and then Amanda, Tabatha, and Mrs. Steppin all in a clump, bringing in with them what seemed like half the snow and several Tupperware containers full of food.

Next arrived something of a surprise.

"Paul?" Margery asked as soon as she opened the door. Paul Rutherford was a longtime family friend. The way she heard it, Paul had known her mom and dad years and years ago, back when they were still together and her dad still lived in England.

Paul was one of Margery's favorite people in the world. She thought of him like a substitute dad or weird uncle. And so it wasn't odd that he was there, really; nor was it odd that he'd arrived with his loyal and ever-present dog, Ranger. But it was odd that he was dressed in slacks and a long, dapper black coat, had combed his hair, had actually shaved, and was carrying a bouquet of roses.

"Hey bug," he said stepping into the hall. He smoothed out his coat and hair a bit self-consciously. "Where's your mom?"

He patted her head absently and wandered off to where they could hear Cynthia's laughter. Margery barely had a moment to puzzle over this, because then, the doorbell rang yet again, and in came Patrick, his boyfriend, Kent, and Alexa.

"It's bloody freezing out there! I can't feel my—"

"Roasted nuts?" J.P. asked at just the wrong time. He'd stepped into the little hallway holding out a bowl of sweet roasted chestnuts.

Once everyone had arrived, it was clear the entire group couldn't fit at the six-person dining table, so they all loaded their plates as little or as much as they liked, and headed into the living room. There, a fire was burning merrily and Christmas music was playing lightly from the radio next to the T.V.

At Amanda's request, they all began their meals in silence. They noticed how their food looked, smelled, tasted, and felt. They were totally present. It was beautiful. It was perfect—

It was way too serious for a party.

It started with Margery. She was making weird squelching noises every time she chewed to see how long it took Emma to laugh. But instead, Jordan on her other side kept looking around the room trying to figure out where the noise was coming from, and eventually seemed to decide it was coming Paul's dog.

At his look of utter confusion and concern for the poor dog, Margery couldn't help it—she burst out laughing, and with that, spit a huge chunk of cornbread right at Jordan, which bounced off his shoulder and was promptly snatched up and eaten, mid-air, by Ranger. Then all was lost, and the room dissolved into laughter.

They continued the rest of the meal, still mindfully, but chatted and laughed with each other. Occasionally, Margery heard her friends saying something like "Hey, cookies are a triggering food for me. I'd like to have one, though. Can I get your support if I feel guilty?" or "I'm feeling a little anxious in a crowd and I want your support if I emotionally eat," or even "I need support in eating enough dinner. When I'm in a situation where I don't have much control, I tend to try not to eat as much as I want or need." She'd never felt prouder to be a part of such an honest group.

After dinner, Margery felt so satisfied. She was full, somewhat sleepy, and surrounded by laughing friends, snowed in and warm. For a tiny moment, her thoughts went into PAMC mode when she bent forward and she realized the waistband on her jeans was way tighter than it had been in weeks, or even that night. She could feel where it dug into her stomach, and immediately, reached for the area with her hand, as though to pinch it or criticize it further.

But just then, Emma leaned her head back and rested it on Margery's shoulder. She could feel the movements of Emma's jawbone whenever she laughed or talked. She brought her attention back to the details of the moment—the room, the smells, the sights, her breath, the tingling sensation in her hands of simply being alive— and suddenly her weight didn't seem to matter so much.

As she looked around the room, focusing on everything going on "outside" of herself, she realized, more than ever, that there was no real "outside" and "inside." This world—she was a part of it, and it was a part of her.

As she watched Tabatha laugh and carelessly take a bite of a cookie, with J.P. applauding her,

As she saw her mother lean her body back to rest against Paul's, and he wrapped his arms around her middle,

She watched Ms. Steppin and Amanda deep in conversation,

Jordan, Alexa, and James looking through the shelf of movies, pointing at different titles here and there,

And Patrick and his love, Kent, holding each other, their eyes closed in contentment, sitting in front of the fire—

She felt, for the first time, like she got it. This was life. This was all that mattered.

Love

Connection

This was her, on her deepest level.

It was everyone and everything.

It was—

Her Inner Self.

(That's me.)

and they all lived happily ever after... for the most part

Here's the truth about happiness: it's an emotion, just like sadness, or anger, or excitement. It comes and it goes in waves.

So when I tell you *they all lived happily ever after*, what I mean is: they all *lived*. They stayed present (most of the time) and felt their emotions. Sadness, happiness, joy, excitement, anger, hurt, jealousy, loneliness—if they'd learned one thing that year in their group, it was: stay present. Grow. Feel it all.

Margery certainly did.

By the time she was getting ready to graduate from school, she had not only taken over the reins of SLBL, but had started another group in their town for people of all ages who needed support with self-esteem, body image, and food. It became such a safe space, people from the next town over and the next town after that heard about it and came to meetings.

The local media picked up on its success and featured this remarkable teenager named Margery in their papers and morning shows.

Like all waves, this one rose and fell, and after all the media attention, Margery was soon out of the spotlight and back to living a normal life. But when she started applying to universities to study psychology, she was awarded a scholarship for her impact on her community.

These days, our friend Margery lives in London with her fiancé, a Miss Laurel Polansky. She works as a Child and Teen Psychologist. She specializes in food and body image issues, and while she hasn't had the urge to throw up or starve herself in many years, she does still sometimes struggle with the image she sees in the mirror. Of course, other days she thinks she looks super-hot. But there's always an up and a down.

Margery

From almost the moment her mom, Cynthia, had to alter her lifestyle and diet for her daughter, she felt relieved. A weight of control was lifted from her shoulders. She finally had a reason to stop controlling her food and her life so, so carefully.

Once she finally let go, she realized what she'd been controlling all along: her feelings. Her feelings of love for her daughter, her feelings of love for herself, and apparently, too, her feelings for one Paul Rutherford. That night at the party, she allowed herself to eat what she wanted, and feel what she truly felt—and had felt for years, but had hidden.

Today, she and Paul live together with two big dogs in that same town, which these days, is not quite so small. They co-teach a cooking class at the nearby community college twice a week, and see Margery and Laurel almost every Sunday for dinners.

Cynthia   ...and Paul

As for Emma, she ended up moving to the states after school and studying at NYU. She and Margery keep in touch—a phone call here, an email there—but mostly, her life is in New York. She has a group of friends. She works for a nonprofit in Manhattan, which brings creative programs to schools. In fact, one day not too long ago a Miss Nipa Chaterjee, who you might remember, gave a talk about meditation and art to one of her schools. They never have realized their connection.

Emma

Amanda, after about ten years, finally stopped caring as much what others thought of her. She told her parents to stop putting so much pressure on her and finally started living the way she wanted to. The way her body wanted to. And as it turns out, her body naturally wants to be about 15 pounds heavier—and for the first time in her life, without constantly dieting, exercising obsessively, and just letting her body do what it naturally wants to—she feels confident.

Amanda

Ms. Steppin is no longer Ms. Steppin at all. No, she didn't get married. She went back to school and became Dr. Steppin. These days, she works with underprivileged kids in London who need, but can't afford, medical help.

Dr. Steppin

Tabatha got better, and got worse, and better, and worse, until a few months ago her family decided she needed more intensive treatment. She was admitted to an eating disorder in-patient program—the finest in Europe—and has just moved back in with her parents until she feels ready to be on her own. She has a cat named Henry who is very supportive.

Tabatha

Henry

Patrick and Kent, believe it or not, are one of those high school couples that actually stayed together. They live, today, in Northern California with their two French bulldogs, a goldfish named Mikey, and are eagerly awaiting the arrival of their new, adopted baby, Gabby.

Patrick   Kent

Jordan, of course, has taken his leadership skills to new heights. In school, he studied Spanish and today lives near Madrid with his girlfriend, Ana. Together, they run a co-op and self-sustaining farm.

¡Hola!

Jordan

J.P.'s acne eventually cleared up and wouldn't you know it, today he is the face of a very prominent designer's aftershave line. (You've totally seen him.)

J.P.

James and J.P., though a couple of years apart, became friends later on in school through the SLBL group, and these days, James and J.P.'s sister, Hanna, live in Chicago both working as journalists. James, by the way, finally filled out when he was about 20. He never did get into sports, though, much to his dad's chagrin.

Sorry, Dad!

James

Alexa works in the same small town where she grew up. She still struggles with emotional eating when things get rough, as many adults do for the rest of their lives. It's not bad, and it's not good. It's just the way it is.

Alexa

Jenny, as you'll remember, was upset at a young age about how girls were treated by boys. Well Jenny took that anger and turned it into action. She now heads one of the biggest feminist publishing companies in the world and runs a website (which I'm sure you've heard of), where women can support each other in business and life. You go, girl!

Jenny

And as for Mrs. Sherman, well, just a few years after our story ended, Mrs. Sherman retired. She decided that yes, in fact, she was getting older. But rather than let it hold her back, she decided to let it move her forward—specifically to a place that she and her husband had fallen in love with on a certain little trip to the Canary Islands, where they still live today.

So there you are: your happily ever after... for the most part.

extras, whatnots, and general whozits

K, I'm a picture!

This is the part in the book where I give you a quick rundown of some of the important stuff I covered in the story, and also some fun little extras that you can check out when you get a chance. These pages will help you, guide you, and generally inspire you to live a more body-positive life.

You are perfect. If you keep thinking about perfection as an actual, physical thing, you know you'll never be perfect. Someone will always be skinnier, fitter, better looking. Even if you're a supermodel. But You are perfect. That's You with a capital Y. The real You.

You are not your body. Think of your body as your greatest tool. It is how You interact with the world. It's how you can move around. Talk to people. Sing. Dance. Paint. Write. But you are not your body.

What are you then? You are Life. Pure Energy. Pure Love. You're star stuff. You, in short, are me and I am You, and I can tell you, you're pretty miraculous just as you are.

It's not really about your body. When you get angry at your thighs for being jiggly, or mad at your face for breaking out, or just hate your tummy—it's usually about something else. So ask yourself, what emotion are you trying not to feel when you start attacking your body? What is really bothering you? Because chances are, it's something else entirely.

Food Stuff = Emotion Stuff. Usually when you eat uncontrollably, you are trying to numb some pain. When you are starving yourself, or severely restricting what you eat—you are trying to control something else in your life, that you feel is out of control. So ask yourself: What are you trying to numb? What are you really trying to control?

Staying Present is Key. Staying present just means being in the moment. Not thinking about the past or future all the time. You can practice this with meditation (I'll include some good ones in the back.) You can do this by just noticing things and people and sounds and smells in the room. Watching your breath. Really paying attention when you eat.

You're not alone. Not only am I here, but there are kids around you right now, I guarantee it, who are going through the same thing. Talk to them. Seek support. There are some things you just can't do alone, and while this book is a start, if you need to talk to someone, do it. Now! I'll wait.

Did you find someone to talk to? A parent? A friend? A counselor? A group? Because it'll help.

I've said it once and I'll say it again:

Don't sweat the small stuff.

It's all small stuff.

body Scanning Meditation

Here we have a simple and fast way to just feel into your body. Feel what's up. What's there. What feels good, what feels bad.

Find a quiet place where you won't be disturbed, or throw on some headphones. You can do this sitting comfortably or even laying down. Close your eyes. And just notice.

You'll start with the tips of our toes. Feel the tingling. The life there. Are they warm? Cold? Comfortable? Relaxed? Just notice them.

Then begin to notice the ball of your foot, and then your heel. Notice the feeling of blood pulsing through your veins. Of Life just coursing through you.

Move on to your ankles, then your calves and your shins.

Notice your knees—how they bend; how they support your strong legs. Feel them fully.

Move on to your thighs and hamstrings. Your hips.

Keep moving all the way up your body, through each little part, and even each little piece of your face, until you reach the very top of your head.

Feel your whole body from the tips of your toes to the top of your head. Feel how it tingles with life. Feel the joy of being alive—even if there is pain or discomfort.

Just feel it. Sit just simply feeling what it feels like to be in a body for 10-20 minutes per day. Your body will thank you for it.

body gratitude Meditation

♥ Go to a quiet place where you won't be disturbed for about 10 minutes. Start by breathing in and out, in and out, and simply observing your breath. After several minutes, once you're good and relaxed, move your attention from your breath onto the area of your heart. Feel it beating. Listen, see if you can hear it. Focus all of your attention on that steady rhythm and then begin to think about all of the things in your life that you're grateful for—the people, the events, the feelings, and the things.

With that gratitude feeling still in your heart, begin to think of all the things you are grateful for about your body. Whether it's your strength, your ability to move around, laugh, or even just read this and sit for this exercise—these are all things you can only do because of your remarkable body.

Let the images float across your mind while you're still focusing your attention on your heart. Feel your heart swell and glow with the joy that all of those things bring you.

Do this once or twice a day, and see how your whole world shifts.

Self-Love Meditation

Find a comfortable place to sit. Plug in some headphones, or make sure you'll have quiet for a few minutes.

Take a few deep breaths in and out, and silently observe the flow of your breath as it enters and leaves. No need to judge it or change it. Just watch it.

Now focus your attention on your heart, and as you breathe in, feel your heart opening and growing warm and soft. As you breathe out, imagine that you are breathing out tension and stress.

Now imagine yourself. Your body. Your face. Imagine that you can place that image inside your heart. And ask your heart "May I be freed from self-doubt. May I love myself."

Keep breathing into your heart and the image of yourself, warmth and love. As you breathe out, release tension and stress.

When you feel at peace and finished, take a deep breath and just let it go.

Repeat this as often as you find helpful.

don't Numb that Negativity Meditation

Clever name, I know. But we've all been there, right? (Right??) NEGATIVITY

Something is upsetting us, but rather than face the real issue, we go for a box of cookies, we starve ourselves, or we beat ourselves up for the way we look.

So instead of doing that, try this: next time something is bothering you, go to a place you won't be disturbed for about 10 minutes. Sit down comfortably and start by breathing in and out, in and out, and just watching your breath without trying to control it.

Now start to think about the thing that is upsetting you. Imagine what happened—play the scene out like it is a movie. See what you saw, hear what you heard, and feel what you felt.

The first step to dealing with the emotion is identifying it. What does this feel like? Is it anger? Sadness? Maybe you're just confused. Whatever it is, give it a name.

Now put your attention back on your body. Can you feel where this emotion is inside you? Really focus now. When you find that spot (or spots) inside you that are hurting or uncomfortable, say out loud "It hurts here." Point to it. Then just focus on that spot, picture it in your mind, and breathe in and out. With every breath out, imagine that you're blowing away that pain in your body.

Sometimes it helps to even stick your tongue out like a dog and just go "AHHHHHHHHH!" Trust me, the sillier you feel doing it, the better you'll feel after.

Now that you've breathed it all out, imagine whatever it was that upset you again. If it was a person, imagine that you could speak to that person. What would you say to them?

Say it out loud, or even write it down on the next page if that helps you. Then turn the page, put it away, and put it out of your head. There's no need to keep thinking about what upset you.

Negativity Scribble Pages

Write down, draw, or simply scribble away whatever you're feeling on these next few pages. Get it all out— don't worry, nobody will see it but you. When you're done, do what you want with the pages: throw them out, crumple them into a ball, tear them up. Just imagine that as you write down these thoughts and feelings, you are ridding them from yourself. And doesn't that feel better!

journal Pages

Dear Diary,

Here's the part in the book where you write the story. You can write about your day. Your crush. Your parents. Whatever you want—this is the place to get it all out. Don't worry, I won't tell a soul. (And you don't have to either.)

Cognitive behavioral therapy

(Adapted from *Mind Over Mood* by Dennis Greenberger & Christine A. Padesky)

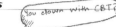

I know this sounds boring — and okay, it is more boring than most of the stuff in here. BUT, the thing is, Cognitive Behavioral Therapy, or CBT, works! Especially for those struggling with food stuff.

So check it out. In the table below, you'll work through a situation, so you can see firsthand how sometimes your thoughts are just thoughts—and they're simply not true.

In **Situation**, write down an event that made you upset, or maybe made you feel uncomfortable, or feel a desire to eat a box of cookies, or even not eat at all. Write down who you were with, what you were doing, when it was, and where it was.

For **Moods**, write down your mood or emotions during the situation.

In **Automatic Thoughts**, answer these questions:

What was going through your mind just before you started to feel this way?

What does this say about you?

What does this mean about you? Your life? Your future?

What are you afraid might happen?

What is the worst thing that could happen if this is true?

What does this mean about how the other person feels/thinks about me?

Now circle the thought here that feels the "hottest" or most alive for you.

In **Evidence that Supports the Hot Thought** you'll look at the circled Hot Thought in the previous column. What **factual** evidence do you have that this is true?

In **Evidence that Does NOT Support the Hot Thought** you'll write down the evidence that this thought is NOT true.

Finally, you'll write down an **Alternative/More Balanced Thought.**

And in the last column, write down how you feel at the end of the exercise.

Try to do these CBT exercises right after or even during the triggering situation.

Situation	Moods	Automatic Thoughts	Evidence that Supports the Hot Thought	Evidence that does NOT support the Hot Thought	Alternative/ More Balanced Thoughts	Your Mood Now

Situation	Moods	Automatic Thoughts	Evidence that Supports the Hot Thought	Evidence that does NOT support the Hot Thought	Alternative/ More Balanced Thoughts	Your Mood Now

Situation	Moods	Automatic Thoughts	Evidence that Supports the Hot Thought	Evidence that does NOT support the Hot Thought	Alternative/ More Balanced Thoughts	Your Mood Now

Containment box

Here's a cool activity for those of you who like making stuff—and who doesn't like making stuff?

It's called a containment box, and it's a physical place to put all your feelings that you just can't handle right now. You can just grab any old box—a shoe box will do—and decorate the outside with pictures and text and anything you'd like, representing the way you think you look to the outside world. Decorate the inside of the box with anything you'd like, showing how you see yourself on the inside.

Then, whenever you have feelings that you simply can't handle right now, write them down on a strip of paper, and stick them in that box.

a letter to your body

Write a letter to your body about all the cool things it does for you and what you're thankful for. If you like, you can even write an apology to your body if you've been treating it rough, like Margery did.

a letter from your body

Write a letter from your body to yourself about how it feels it has been treated by you and the world.

a letter to food

Hi Food,

Write a letter to food about all the cool things it does for you and what you're thankful for. If you like, you can even write an apology to food if you've been treating it rough.

a letter from food

Write a letter from food to yourself about how it feels it has been treated by you and the world.

dEAR SElf, ← (Food: Not the best with writing)

Mirror, Mirror Exercise

Write "I LOVE AND ACCEPT MYSELF NO MATTER WHAT" on a piece of paper and tape it to your mirror. Tell this to yourself every day, twice a day, for three weeks. See how your life changes.

List of body gratitudes

Earlier we did a body gratitude meditation, and here's the part where you actually write your body gratitudes down. Why? Because science shows that writing things down has this magical way of really drilling them into your brain, and changes the way you think and live much faster.

On the next page, I want you to list out at least three things you're grateful for about your body. Each day, come back to this page, and write down at least three new things. If it sounds hard, remember:

- Your body is what lets you move through the world
- It lets you laugh
- It lets you create
- It lets you read this awesomeness
- It even lets you have friends and family

So go on. What has your body done for you lately?

authentic relating games

Adapted from the Authentic
Relating Games Manual by Sara Ness

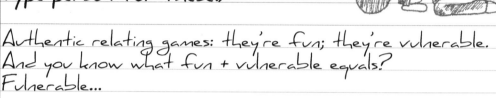

(You'll need a timer and a parent-
type-person for these.)

Authentic relating games: they're fun; they're vulnerable.
And you know what fun + vulnerable equals?
Fulnerable...

But also, it equals a good way to get to know yourself
and the person you're playing with better, faster. I
recommend playing with a parent figure—whether that's
an actual mom or dad, aunt, uncle, grandparent, teacher.
You know. Some person who's older than you that you
trust. Once you've tried that, you can also play these
games with your peers that you trust.

But play them with people you trust with your emotions.
Because they're designed to open you and your partner
up like a can-opener.

In a good way!

Noticing Game

Directions: With a parent/parent, choose one person to
be A and one to be B. A, you'll begin by saying: "Sitting
here with you, I notice..." and talk about something in
your experience of that moment. B then responds:
"Hearing that, I notice . . ." Go back and forth with
"Hearing that I notice..." for two-five minutes. The
things B notices don't have to be related to what A

notices; the wording is just meant to show that there is a relationship here between you two.

Empathy

Directions: With a partner/parent, sit down, and take a few seconds to just sit there making eye contact. I know, it sounds weird. But it's also powerfully connecting. Choose who's A and who's B. Then, A, you'll have two minutes to share something that's really on your mind or weighing on your heart. Afterward, B, take one minute to share exactly what you heard—just the facts, with as little interpretation as possible.

A, you'll then say what you said again, clarify it, or add in anything you left out, for two minutes. Then, for two minutes, B, share what you felt while listening to the whole thing and what you think you now understand about A. Then switch roles and do it again.

Trading Faces

Directions: With a parent/partner, choose an "A" and a "B." Sit in silence for a about a minute just to sink in to the moment. Then, person A, imagine how you must seem to person B. If you were looking at your own face and body, your own words and body movements, how would it look from the outside? How would B feel about them?

Share by saying: "I must seem..." or "I must look..." and describe, for two-four minutes.

Once the time is up, B, you'll share your feedback for two-three minutes. You can say: "To me you seem..." "To me you look..." "I felt you the most honestly when you said..." "I felt _____ being with you..."

The Appreciation Game

You might recognize this game as the one Margery and Emma played. Here's how it works:

Directions: With a parent/partner, choose an object in the room you're in. Together, notice everything you appreciate about it—what does it look like? Feel like? Smell like? What color is it? How does it make you feel? Do this for two-three minutes. Then close your eyes, and notice what it feels like to appreciate something.

Then you guys will choose another object. Do this whole thing again for two-three minutes.

Then you guys will look at each other. Person A will say out loud everything they notice and appreciate about person B for two-three minutes.

Then person B will tell person A everything that they notice and appreciate about them for two-three minutes.

Finally, end the game by sitting with your eyes closed for one minute, just feeling what it feels like to appreciate and be appreciated.

Love and Self-Love

Directions: With your parent/partner, choose who will be
A and who will be B. A, you'll tell B all about a person that
you love for three-five minutes. You'll tell B why you love
this person (or even pet), what you love about him or her.
Really feel how much you love this being while you talk.

Then B, you'll take three-four minutes to share how this all
made you feel.

A, you'll then talk about why you love yourself with just
as much love and care and feeling and sympathy as you did
before when talking about that person/creature you love
so much.

Then again, person B, you'll share back how that made you
feel.

Next time you play the game, switch roles.

Some Sentence Stems

Sentence stems are super easy and pretty much exactly what they sound like. With your partner (Mom, Dad, friend, family member, preferably not your dog who as much as I love your dog, can't really help here), you'll take turns starting a sentence with the words below, and fill in the rest yourself.

For example, with the sentence stem: **I feel scared to tell you...**

You might say "I feel scared to tell you... how much I care about you."

Or, "I feel scared to tell you... I accidentally broke your glasses."

Go back and forth just focusing on **one** sentence stem for two-three minutes. Then you can move on and pick a new one.

Okay, you got it. Here are some helpful stems to work with:

How I feel about my body is...

I think others see my body as...

Something I wish more people knew about me is...

What I think you think of me is...

What if...?

One of the best experience I've ever had in my body is...

One of the hardest experiences I've ever had in my body is...

If you really knew me, you would know...

Something I appreciate about you is...

Something I appreciate about me is...

What I think when I look in the mirror is...

Something I feel in my body right now is...

healthy food stuff for real

Here's the deal about food: It's tricky. As you probably know more than most people, food can be kind of addictive. I mean, people use it all the time as a way to escape feelings, as something to do when they're bored or uncomfortable, or even by limiting food in order to pretend they have control over their life!

(Spoiler Alert: nobody actually has complete control of their life. Life just happens. So, you know, might as well let that one go now...)

The thing is, people have to eat food! I know. Duh, right? But unlike alcohol or cigarettes or other addictive things, you can't just quit eating because it can be hard. Food is what gives you life! It's what allows your heart to beat, your lungs to breathe, your mind to think!

So it's pretty great. And if you struggle with food, it may not always be easy. And I highly suggest finding a nutritionist and a counselor to talk to if food is really emotional for you (it is for a lot of people.)

But this should at least be a good place to start.

Food is fuel.

You need food to power your brain to get good grades. You need it to run and play outside. You need it to participate in sports. To hang out with friends. To dance. To read. To laugh. You need food for every single thing you will ever do—so make sure you're putting good fuel in your body.

You are what you eat.

I know, people have been saying this forever, but it's true. In Chinese medicine, in fact, food is medicine and medicine is food, because they believe quite literally, you are what you eat. If you eat chicken, you'll develop the energy of a chicken. If you eat fish, you'll develop the energy of fish.

Whether or not you subscribe to such a literal philosophy on food, you do know that you are what you eat. You know it because of the way you feel after eating a bowl of sugary ice cream, versus a bowl of vegetables and brown rice. You can feel which one works for you.

Do that 80/20 Thing

Here's a little rule that I've seen help a lot of my peeps: The 80/20 rule. You eat healthy, yummy, good foods 80 percent of the time; then 20 percent, you treat yoself! Life is meant to be enjoyed—and a healthy balance between delicious healthy food and delicious treats is important.

So what are these healthy foods exactly? Glad you asked.

Everybody should have a mostly plant-based diet. That means, most of the food you eat should be veggie- and fruit-based.

Things like this:

- Arugula
- Asparagus
- Beets

- Bell peppers
- Bok choy
- Broccoli

- Brussels sprouts
- Cabbage
- Carrots
- Cauliflower
- Celery
- Collard greens
- Corn, yellow
- Cucumbers
- Dandelion greens
- Eggplant
- Garlic
- Green beans
- Green peas
- Kale
- Leeks
- Mushrooms
- Mustard greens
- Okra
- Olives
- Onions
- Parsnips
- Potatoes
- Pumpkin
- Romaine lettuce
- Spinach
- Squash, summer
- Squash, winter
- Sweet potatoes
- Swiss chard
- Turnip greens
- Watercress
- Yams
- Zucchini
- Apples
- Avocados
- Bananas

- Blueberries
- Blackberries
- Cranberries
- Grapes
- Guava
- Mangos
- Oranges
- Papaya
- Pomegranates
- Strawberries
- Tomatoes
- Watermelon
- Etc.

Of course you need protein in order to build strong muscles. Go for lean proteins, because they're better for your health, heart, and cholesterol, and will give you more energy than a meat with lots of fat or grease.

That would be, things like this:

- Greek yogurt
- Cottage cheese
- Eggs
- Salmon
- Chicken breast
- Turkey
- Tuna
- Tilapia

And if you're a vegetarian or vegan, don't worry, there's protein for you too:

- Soy bean protein
- Edamame
- Chia Seeds
- Beans
- Lentils
- Hemp seeds
- Ezekiel Bread
- Quinoa
- Eggs (not vegan)
- Hummus
- Spinach
- Almond Butter
- Plant-based protein powder (in a yummy smoothie!)
- Greek yogurt (not vegan)

You'll need good, energizing, healthy whole grains:

- Ezekiel whole grain bread
- Whole oats/oatmeal
- Brown rice
- Bulgur
- Whole Rye
- Couscous
- Quinoa
- Amaranth

And, contrary to what you might have heard: You'll need FAT! Now hold up: not all food fat is created equal. There are healthy fats and unhealthy fats.

Here are some healthy fats you should enjoy:

- Fish! (Salmon, trout, mackerel, tuna, anchovies, sardines, etc. are all packed with healthy Omega-3 fats)
- Plant oils (olive oil, coconut oil, avocado oil, grapeseed oil, hempseed oil)
- Nuts: almonds, cashews, hazelnuts, walnuts, peanuts, Brazil nuts
- (Note: do not eat or touch any of these nuts if you think you might have a nut allergy!)
- Seeds: chia seeds, hemp seeds, sunflower seeds, pumpkin seeds, sesame seeds
- Avocado
- Olives
- Coconut meat

Here are some not-so-healthy fats, you might want to **avoid**:

- Trans fats: chips, crackers, French fries, packaged cookies, any hydrogenated oils

- Saturated Fats: Butter, cream sauces, high fat cheese, chicken fat, beef fat, pork fat, lamb fat, milk chocolate, hot dogs, sausage, ice cream, whole milk

- Cholesterol: High fat meats & high fat dairy products

Girls in particular: you guys need a pretty good amount of **healthy fat** in your diet, in order to produce the hormones you need for puberty. (Oh don't you worry—we're talking about that next!) But guys, you need healthy fats too. Healthy fats like the ones listed above are needed for everyone to keep your brain working, to keep your heartbeat strong, and to keep your body working.

Think of healthy fats as the lubrication for the machine that is your body. If you don't give it healthy fats, nothing else is going to work properly. (And heads up: If you think cutting fat out of your diet will help you lose weight— think again. You need healthy fats in order to properly digest food!!)

When you eat mostly vegetables, fruits, plus whole grains, lean proteins, and healthy fats, your body will feel so strong. Your brain will feel super-powered. And when you do decide to have a cookie or treat, it will taste so much better.*

Remember: 80/20.

How many calories should you eat per day? Don't even worry about calories—the amount of calories you need is totally different from what someone else needs and it changes from day to day. Just pay attention to ingredients. Avoid things with:

- Processed sugar
- Fried foods
- Unhealthy fats & grease
- Ingredients whose names you can't even pronounce
- Preservatives
- White flour
- Artificial sweeteners
- Artificial colors or ingredients

And you, my friend, will be golden.

Oh Yeah... that awkward Page about Puberty...

Okay, this is weird for me too, guys. So I'll keep this short, since I know you're probably already getting these "talks" in Health Class.

But there are some things you need to know about puberty and your body—and even food.

When you get to be anywhere from about eight to 15, guys and gals, your brain will start releasing a little hormone called the gonadotropin-releasing hormone, or GnRH. When this stuff hits your pituitary gland (which is nestled nicely right under your brain), that gland starts releasing two more hormones: LH (or luteinizing hormone, though why you'd ever want to remember this, I don't know) and FSH (follicle-stimulating hormone. Obvs.)

You guys and girls both have these hormones, and depending on if you're a guy or girl, they'll effect you differently.

Guys

These hormones will course right through your blood and give your testicles the signal to start producing testosterone and sperm. The testosterone will do all those fun things like:

- Make your voice get lower
- Make the hair on your body thicker
- Give you hair in some new, interesting places
- Gift you with pimples on your face, chest, and perhaps back

- Make you like a foot taller in a matter of months
- Make you gain weight
- Make your shoulders broader
- Could make your breasts bigger (yes, for guys!)

Girls

For the ladies, during puberty those two hormones we talked about begin telling your ovaries to start producing estrogen. This little hormone will be around for a long time in your life, doing all sorts of fun things to get your body ready for pregnancy*.

*Note: this does not mean that you have to get pregnant. Ever. It's your body and your choice whether or not you want to have a baby someday, and plenty of women choose not to have kids at all. You do you, girl.

During puberty, though, many girls think they should start dieting, because they'll notice:

- Increased body fat
- Oily skin and/or pimples/acne
- Hips widening
- Breasts getting bigger
- Butt getting bigger

Of course, as you know, your body needs all the nutrients it can get during puberty, so going on a diet isn't a good idea. You are supposed to gain weight during this time—and when this is and how it is is different for every girl out there.

It's a magical time! And it totally sucks.

Don't worry, I'm here for you.

Consent

This, my friends, we could talk about for an entire book. But for now, I just want to introduce the idea: consent.

Consent is a word with a lot of meanings, but here, we're talking about it in relation to bodies.

Always ask permission

If you want to hug someone or touch someone, ask their permission.

No means No

Did the girl you wanted to hug or kiss say no? Then I promise you, she didn't mean "maybe." She meant no. If the boy said he didn't want to be slapped on the butt or punched in the shoulder—he meant no. So when someone says no, you better listen.

Not everyone is as physical as you are

If you and your parents are very huggy and affectionate, it might come as a surprise to you that not everyone interacts this way. Be sure to ask permission, listen for a yes or no, and you know, get to know someone before you go around hanging all over them. Some people love physical affection—and for some people, it's uncomfortable.

Manly Men: So 10 Years ago

These days it's becoming so clear that our old definitions of being a "man," where all guys are dudes and have chest hair and are strong and play on the football team and love women—well, those are a thing of the past.

Gender norms are so 15 years ago.

Guys reading this—it's your body, you do what you want with it. If you want to dance, to write, to sing to act, to play outside, to climb trees, to cry, to feel, to swim, to do yoga, to dress up in skirts and heels, to put on makeup, to identify as whatever gender you prefer! To truly live fully, you have to be brave and be yourself. Don't worry what anyone else thinks.

And as for being lady-like...

Borrrrring! The days are long gone of women having to wear skirts and dresses every day. Where girls couldn't play sports, or get muddy, go camping, get whatever job they want to, or even run for president.

You girls—this is your body. It's your choice. You get to decide who gets to touch it, or look at it, or talk about it. YOU get to decide whether or not you like men, or women, or neither. YOU get to decide whether or not you want to have a baby someday, or get married, or climb a freaking volcano! The point here is: You are you. You can make that whatever in your wildest dreams you want to.

If you're reading this, guy, girl, neither, or both: you can do anything. You can do everything. You are so strong.

With your body: your tool for interacting with this world.

You can do it all.

And if things ever get overwhelming, don't worry.

I got your back.

Stuff Smart People have Said

I think of all the years I've wasted hating myself fat, wanting myself thin. Feeling guilty about every croissant, then giving up carbs, then fasting, then dieting, then worrying when I wasn't dieting, then eating everything I wanted until the next diet. All that energy I could have spent loving what is.
  - Oprah Winfrey

My limbs work so I'm not going to complain about the way my body is shaped.
  - Drew Barrymore

Once I stopped worrying so much about what other people thought about me, I was finally free to be me and look like me.
  - Amanda Wallace

I was not ladylike, nor was I manly. I was something else altogether. There were so many different ways to be beautiful.
  - Michael Cunningham

Among my acquaintances there is no woman wearing Extra Small. No, sorry, there is one: my daughter. The point is, my daughter is 11 years old.
  - Kate Winslet

Being Size 0 is a career in itself, so we shouldn't try and be like them. It's not realistic and it's not healthy.
  - Rihanna

At 27, I'm able to admit I don't like my body. But it shouldn't have taken me years to get to that point. I spent too long feeling like I had a secret, that I was hiding my weight issues, unable to talk about it, because rules of masculinity forbid it. It shouldn't be extraordinary for men to talk about their bodies.
  - Tyler Kingkade

Even I don't wake up looking like Cindy Crawford.
  - Cindy Crawford

Is fat really the worse thing a human being can be? Is fat worse than vindictive, jealous, shallow, vain, boring, evil, or cruel? Not to me.
  - J.K. Rowling

Comparing your body to that of a celebrity is totally unrealistic. I've interviewed dozens of celebrities about their fitness regimens for movie roles and to call it "extreme" is an understatement. It's months of brutal training, dietary deprivation, dehydration, contouring makeup and great lighting for one short scene. It's painful - and unsustainable.
  - James Fell

Take your time and your talent and figure out what you have to contribute to this world. And get over what the hell your butt looks like in those jeans!
  - America Ferrera

I definitely have body issues, but everybody does. When you come to the realization that everybody does — even the people that I consider flawless — then you can start to live with the way you are.
  - Taylor Swift

You have to look past it—you look how you look, and be comfortable. What are you going to do? Be hungry every single day to make other people happy? That's just dumb.
  - Jennifer Lawrence

Stop wasting so much energy hating your body; it makes you weaker. Everything good in your life begins from the moment you begin accepting, understanding, respecting and loving your true self.
  - Harry Papas

The male stereotype makes masculinity not just a fact of biology but something that must be proved and re-proved, a continual quest for an ever-receding Holy Grail.
  - Marc Feigen Fasteau

Amazing people come in every size. Never let anyone tell you that you're worth less because you're taller, shorter, wider, or rounder than someone else. Your size doesn't define you, your actions do.
  - Bruce Sturgell

When I realized I was trying to control my emotions by controlling my food, I could finally let go. And you know what? Feeling your emotions—every single one of them—is the only way to truly live.
  - Our girl, Margery

Made in the USA
Middletown, DE
30 July 2017